The Nature of Grace

Ponderings on God's Abundant Grace

by

Linda Elmore Teeple

Dear Judy,

Please accept this gift as a deep "thank you" for honoring exactly what to do and exactly what I wanted. I'm so grateful for your prayers, support and the honor to work with you!

God Bless You —

Charlotte

Psalm 121

March 25, 2008

Available for purchase at lulu.com · http://stores.lulu.com/lindyteep

Book Design © 2006 MRSDesign, Marie R. Stonestreet; www.mrsdesign.com.

ISBN 978-1-4303-0183-7

Acknowledgements

With appreciation to the many people in my life
who have showered me with God's grace, especially:

My husband, Rex
My children, Matt, Beth, and Kristy
My mom, Charlotte Reuman Elmore
My mother-in-law, Marceile Teeple

My friends and colleagues:

Bonnie Cox, Diana Delph, Michael and Christine Elmore, Lea Fifer,
Jake Fisher, Mary Rose Knipp, Vickie Knipp, Rusty Moe, Martha Nalley,
Sandra Overstreet, Susan Sherer-Vincent, Irene Silva, Mary, Sybil, and
James Simpson, Caroline Smith, Beckie Kahl,
Christie Stephens, Andy Stoner, Ruth Anne Teeple, and John Young

A very special thank you to:

John Silvey for lending his artistic talents
to creating the beautiful cover

Marie Stonestreet for her assistance
and guidance in publishing my book

and

my canine companions, who have taught me so
much about God's unconditional love and grace:

Muffin, Midnight, Trixie, and Panda
and Leader Dog puppies, Grace, Hope, and Faith

Thank you for believing in me!

Dedication

To God:

"Who is able to do immeasurably more than all we ask or imagine,
according to his power that is at work within us."
Ephesians 3:20 NIV

And in memory of:

Jason David Teeple, Frank Elmore, Minnie Reuman, and Marjorie Reuman Rettke

The Nature of Grace
Ponderings on God's Abundant Grace

⚘ Table of Contents ⚘

Foreword

Spanish poet, Antonio Machado, says: *"Caminante, no hay camino. Se hace camino al andar.* Traveler, there is no path. The path is made by walking." By reading this book, you are walking with a master traveler, a woman who would never presume to know the places where you should step, but who, humbly and valiantly, shows you some of the waymarks on her own path.

The pieces in this little book—like flecks of ruby, amethyst, or carnelian--remind me that God woos. And grace is the language of God's wooing. Grace speaks in the visible loam of life—trees, seasons, relationships; and in the invisible—hope, exile, rejection, yearning, bliss. Linda Teeple's pearlescent descriptions of grace soothe and challenge me. I am inspired; that is *infused with encouragement, animated, stimulated; I sense a divine influence upon my soul.*

I need this book. I need it because I live in an accelerated, superficial world where personality is enriched and encouraged at the expense of the inner life; where self-concern leads to fear and multi-tasking leads to exhaustion. I need this book because I forget that, to faithfully walk my own path on the earth, I must become transparent to the transcendent, which--in the heart-deep words of the psalmist--*daily loadeth us with benefits.*

The Nature of Grace is the first-fruits of Linda Teeple's path of service. Read it—and leap.

Rusty C. Moe,
author of **Our Presence Together In Chaos** and **Where God Learns**

Introduction

Preface

"The world is charged with the grandeur of God."[1]

*I*n 1996, I began writing about grace and have not put down my pen since. Reared in the Lutheran church, I learned about grace within *the* denomination that has *the* scoop on grace. It was, after all, Martin Luther[2] who stumbled over "by grace you have been saved…" (Ephesians 2:8 NIV) and revolutionized the church.

My mother repeatedly told me about God's grace, love, and forgiveness, and sat on the edge of my bed many a night as I agonized over, "Am I saved?" and, "Am I good enough?" Over the years, I grew in my *intellectual* understanding of grace, but I just didn't "get" it on a *heart* level.

It wasn't until my early forties that I made the heart connection. Quietly, yet profoundly, the arms of Grace opened up and I was at last able to truly understand and accept God's amazing, gracious embrace. Grace had been there all along, of course; I just finally believed that God loved me just the way I was and would go to the ends of the earth to rescue me should I ever stray away from his flock.

Suddenly, all my beliefs about having to earn God's love receded into the background and grace took its rightful place in the foreground of my life. Slowly it dawned on me that God had created me *just* the way he wanted me. He had planted hopes and dreams in my heart and endowed me with the talents and resources to realize them. Having struggled from childhood on with a huge inferiority complex, this was a *very* different way of seeing myself.

---

1 Hopkins, Gerard Manley, Jesuit priest, 1844-1889.
2 The Internet Encyclopedia of Philosophy, www.iep.utm.edu/1/luther.htm.

Grace-Filled Eyes

*P*hilip Yancey states that, "All of us in the church need 'grace-healed eyes' to see the potential in others for the same grace that God has so lavishly bestowed on us. 'To love a person,' said Dostoevsky, 'means to see him as God intended him to be.'"[3]

The Bible calls us to love others *as we love ourselves* (see Matthew 22:39). Thus, we must first turn our grace-filled eyes on ourselves; we must first see ourselves as God sees us. While my gift of grace-sight grew slowly, steadily, imperceptibly, there was one specific moment when my eyes became grace-filled. When I peered into the mirror of my heart, I visualized myself in an amazing new way that prepared me to see all God's creation with new vision.

"Every writer has one main theme," says Yancey, "a spoor that he or she keeps sniffing around, tracking, following it to its source."[4] My spoor is "grace." I write about Grace because I want everyone to "get" grace. I write about Grace because I want everyone to have grace-filled, grace-healed eyes—to see themselves and to see others through God's eyes.

3 Yancey, Philip, <u>What's So Amazing About Grace?</u> Study Guide, Zondervan Publishing House, 1998, p.91.

4 Yancey, Philip, <u>Soul Survivor: How My Faith Survived the Church</u>, Doubleday, 2001, p. 7.

Peripheral Vision

I feel closest to God when I am surrounded by nature. It makes me downright cranky when I am not able to be in the woods, smell the fresh, moist, life-giving earth; listen to the chatter of quarrelsome squirrels, the hum of bugs; catch a glimpse of a hawk soaring above the tree-tops. Nature is like air to me; I need it to feel alive, to find refuge from stress, to hear myself think, to travel to that place within me where God and I walk quietly together. Being in the woods fills me with an indescribable joy, excitement, and contentment.

Just as the ability to see myself through new eyes is tricky, catching sight of God also requires a fine-tuned vision. This is very much like my sightings of wildlife: wispy snatches, caught out of the corner of my eye when I'm least expecting it,

"Nature is like air to me; I need it to feel alive..."

obscured by a haphazard tangle of tree limbs or bushy ground cover. It happens so quickly and catches my breath, and almost before it registers in my brain, the enticing image has flown, leaped, or faded away. I continue to stand quiet and still, my body leaning forward, alert and ready to bound or take flight, my eyes intently searching, straining vainly to peer into the vastness where I cannot follow.

I must be satisfied with my sketchy memory of the elusive images. I am disappointed, yes, but my belief in God's existence and amazing grace quickens my heart and soul, and hope for future sightings is renewed. I am again reassured that my omniscient, omnipresent, omnipotent God is close at hand, in the thickets and tangles of my life, overseeing my every step from the treetops. I stand poised, on tiptoe, in childlike anticipation.

Upon awakening from his amazing dream of angels ascending a staircase to heaven, Jacob uttered, "Surely the Lord is in this place, and I was not aware of it…. How awesome is this place! This is none other than the house of God; this is the gate of heaven" (Genesis 28:16-17 NIV). In response to this passage, Mary Catherine Bateson ponders, "if we believe that such experiences come naturally and are basic to human beings, we may also be opening doors to the recognition of the sacred in ordinary life and in the world around us."[5] While I don't mean to imply that my walks in the woods are akin to Jacob's encounter with God, I couldn't agree with him more! Like Anne Lamott, "I do not understand the mystery of grace, only that it meets us where we are but does not leave us where it found us."[6] In this regard, Jacob, Mary Catherine, Anne, and I are kindred.

---

5 Bateson, Mary Catherine, Peripheral Visions: Learning Along the Way, HarperCollins Publishers, 1994, p. 201. Bateson is the daughter of anthropologist, Margaret Mead, and social scientist, Gregory Bateson.

6 Lamott, Anne, Traveling Mercies: Some Thoughts On Faith, Anchor Books, 1999, p. 143.

I believe that such encounters with grace—whether earthshaking, like Jacob's, or subtle and discreet, like most of mine—happen continuously. "We cannot walk an inch without trying to walk to God,"[7] states Anne Sexton. My excursions in the woods have convinced me of this. While this is true no matter where I am, it is most evident—and I am most open to it—when I am surrounded by towering sycamores, delicate wildflowers, and the crunch of fallen leaves.

---

7 Excerpt from "Not so. Not so.", from <u>The Awful Rowing Toward God</u> by Anne Sexton. Copyright © 1975 by Loring Conant, Jr., Executor of the Estate of Anne Sexton. Reprinted by permission of Houghton Mifflin Company. All rights reserved.

Hope

*N*ature also fills me with hope. In September, our nation observed the fifth anniversary of 9/11. Rarely a day goes by without news of some senseless slaughter of human lives somewhere on this planet. Nature itself gives us mudslides, hurricanes, tsunamis. Human error leads to coal mining accidents, forest fires, and tragic car accidents. Human lives are devastated by world hunger, cancer, sexual assault, domestic violence, prejudice, and persecution... Within my own community, there are children who are dealing with tragic, violent, senseless deaths of parents, and even siblings. Given the pain and devastation surrounding us, and permeating our own lives, it can be terribly difficult to be hopeful. A trek into the woods or a walk on the beach reminds me—if only briefly—that there is life beyond the pain.

"What if nature is speaking to us? What if sunrise and sunset tell the tale everyday, remembering Eden's glory, prophesying Eden's return? ...nature is God's word to us also (Romans 1:20 NIV). If we paid close attention, we would discover something of great joy and wonder: the restoration of the world played out before us each spring and summer is precisely what God is promising us about our lives."[8] How I need those sunrises and sunsets and the changing seasons to remind me that life is secure in God's love and grace!

---

8 Reprinted by permission. The Journey of Desire, John Eldredge, 2000, Thomas Nelson, Inc., Nashville, Tennessee, pp. 108, 112. All rights reserved. Romans 1:20 reads: "For since the creation of the world God's invisible qualities—his eternal power and divine nature—have been clearly seen, being understood from what has been made…"

P
CROSS
I
N
T
S

*I*n 1996, my friend and colleague, Sandra Overstreet, and I opened Crosspoints Counseling Services, Inc., our own Marriage and Family Therapy practice. One day while brainstorming on the phone, we discovered that when you intersect "cross" and "points," it makes a perfect cross. This was confirmation that *Crosspoints* was to be our name and our logo would be this cross.

Crosspoints became a very important metaphor for me and I use it often in my writing to refer to times in our lives when our winding, twisting paths intersect with God's path. We are totally oblivious to most of these intersections, wandering aimlessly and wondering, all the while, "where is God?"

This book is a compilation of my writings on Grace. Most of the essays were originally created for "Pondering the Crosspoints," a column I wrote for my church newsletter for nine years. My inspirations come from scripture passages or quotes that I come across in my reading, or from personal experiences from which I draw a spiritual analogy.

I discover grace in the most bazaar places, in those precious moments of *peripheral vision*. What do Jesus and the Crocodile Hunter have in common? How are spiders, mud, an ass—and yes, even snot—symbols of God's abiding grace? I do worry a bit that some of my readers will experience such metaphors as irreverent, sacrilegious, even blasphemous!

Brennan Manning laments that, "the word itself, *grace*, has become trite and debased through misuse and overuse. It does not move us the way it moved our early Christian ancestors."[9] My objective is to bring a fresh perspective—a very human perspective—on a spiritual mystery that is so hard for many of us pilgrims to grasp and claim. These *Ponderings* spring forth from my heart to the page when God and I cross paths. And sometimes we get a little crazy and silly when we run into each other! My objective is not to convince you of my way of thinking, but rather, to cause you to ponder anew God's abundant grace.

Jesus was a master of metaphor, and I, too, love to create word pictures, bringing Grace within arm's reach of the heart. I invite you now to hike with me into the Nature of Grace, keeping your own *crosspoints* in mind.

Linda Teeple
Fall, 2006

9 Manning, Brennan, The Ragamuffin Gospel, Multnomah Publishers, 2000, p. 20.

Chapter I

"Over the River and through the Woods..."

He who plants a tree, plants a hope.[10]
~ Lucy Larcom

Grace is ...the dynamic outpouring of God's loving nature
that flows into and through creation in an endless self-offering
of healing, love, illumination and reconciliation.[11]
~ Gerald May

In every walk with nature one receives far more than he seeks.
~ John Muir

One touch of nature makes the whole world kin.
~ William Shakespeare

---

10 Larcom, Lucy, poetess and hymn writer, from "Plant a Tree".
11 May, Gerald G., <u>Addiction and Grace: Love and Spirituality in the Healing of Addictions</u>, Harper
    Collins Publishers, 1988.

Like a Tree...

Blessed is the man who[se]...delight is in the law of the Lord
and on his law he meditates day and night. He is like a
tree planted by streams of water, which yields its fruit
in season and whose leaf does not wither.

Psalm 1: 1-3 NIV

*I*n case you haven't noticed yet, I *love* metaphors.
Metaphors are powerful word pictures that help us
grasp and hold onto important truths that guide us
through life. The Bible is full of metaphors. Both
David and Jesus are masters of the metaphor;
David in his poetry and Jesus in his parables.
When I can't find the answers to life's
dilemmas, metaphors seem to help me hang in
there until all the pieces of the puzzle fall into
place (that's one of my favorite metaphors!).
And when all the pieces *still* don't fall into
place, metaphors help me accept the paradoxes,
disappointments and imperfections of my life.

I love to walk in the woods along the river,
and thus the metaphor from Psalm 1, *"like
a tree planted by streams of water which
yields its fruit in season and whose leaf
does not wither,"* speaks vividly to me. On
my walks I see trees in all stages, from seed
pods stuck precariously in the ground, sending
forth their first tender green shoots, to gorgeous
dogwoods in their full spring regalia of blossoms. I've
also seen trees scarred by lightening, yet standing tall, still full of life; trees whose
entire root systems have been washed out from under them—one week I see them
leaning precariously over the White River, and the next week, they have succumbed
to gravity and erosion, their tree tops and branches catching debris flowing down
stream while a few tenacious roots hang on to the eroding bank for dear life.

I am often very much like these trees, scarred, eroded, hanging on to life by a few
"roots." A very important part of my root system is my faith in God. His Word. He
is my "streams of water" who keeps me from withering. Isn't that a *great*
metaphor? I need to remember this when it truly seems like I am withering—when
I feel spiritually, mentally, and/or emotionally zapped. These are the times when I
need to remember *where* I am planted and just hang on. **Water is on the way!**

The Hollow

Search me, O God, and know my heart; test me and know my
anxious thoughts. See if there is any offensive way in me,
and lead me in the way everlasting.
Psalm 139:23-24 NIV

"*N*o, Panda! No!" It's a crisp winter afternoon and Panda and I are just beginning a walk in the woods. Panda has dashed out of sight to the east, bounds momentarily back into sight, turns abruptly and heads south. As she circles back toward me, her nose picks up an irresistible scent. Shifting into hunting mode, centuries of retriever instinct coursing though her body, nose to the ground, Panda zeros in on an old tree.

In a hollow about a foot above the ground, Panda has discovered a sleepy raccoon. Barking excitedly, tail wagging wildly, Panda pokes her nose into the hollow and attempts to paw her way toward the prize. She circles the tree several times, looking for another route, but returns to the opening and repeats her poking and scratching.

"No! Panda! No!" I shout frantically and race toward her. Pulling Panda away from the opening, my eyes adjusting to the reduced light, I can just barely make out the image of a curled-up raccoon groggily peering back at us. Ever since this discovery, Panda and I have been checking out all the hollows we can find in hopes of finding other creatures.

It's funny how when you become fascinated with something, suddenly you find the object of your interest popping up in surprising places. As I was reading Wilderness Wanderings: A Lenten Pilgrimage, I delighted in the author's use of the metaphor of the hollow. Marilyn Brown Oden invites the Lenten pilgrim to "peer into that small hollow at the core of our being" where we can "discover old truths."[12]

One Sunday, my pastor expounded on the importance of acknowledging and facing our shadow side—those troubling aspects of our personality that we prefer to deny. As John spoke, I could picture myself peering into my own shadowy hollow. Lent is traditionally a time when we are called to humbly look within, in the light of the cross. Jesus entered into the darkness – our darkness – as he hung on the cross. With his last breath, he declared, *"It is finished"* (John 19:30). And it is. Finished!

As you take your Lenten pilgrimage within—a pilgrimage you can take at any time—allow the promise of the cross to light your way. This path leads to resurrection—Christ's resurrection and to ours as well. May every morning be Easter morn, and celebrate daily the cleansing power of the cross to transform you and make you new.

---

12 Oden, Marilyn Brown, Wilderness Wanderings: A Lenten Pilgrimage, Upper Room Books, 1995, p. 28.

Living Stones

As you come to him, the living Stone – rejected by men but chosen
by God and precious to him – you also, like living stones, are being
built into a spiritual house to be a holy priesthood, offering spiritual
sacrifices acceptable to God through Jesus Christ.
1 Peter 2:4-5 NIV

I have been reveling in the beauty of spring recently—last week, driving through Tennessee and Georgia where spring is a week or so ahead of us, and this week, here in Indiana where the newborn leaves and bright spring flowers are such a welcome sight. A walk through Mounds State Park yesterday, where a living carpet of wildflowers is gloriously laid by our Creator, confirms that new life abounds. So I'm sure you can understand my lack of enthusiasm as I contemplate writing about a stone. A stone. I love metaphors, but could there be a less exciting, less inspiring metaphor than a stone???

But wait. What's this about a "living" stone? Hmmm… A quick perusing of my Nave's Topical Bible reveals that the stone is used figuratively in numerous passages throughout both the Old and the New Testaments. If my memory serves me right,

"Could there be a less exciting, less inspiring metaphor than a stone???"

Moses once unleashed a fountain of much needed water for the thirsty Israelites by striking a stone—the rock at Horeb (see Exodus 17:1-7). Maybe there is indeed more here than meets the eye.

So what exactly does Peter mean when he says that we are like "living stones"? Is this simply an oxymoron or a rock-solid spiritual truth? I've seen rocks in the woods that have delicate plants sprouting out of crevices where the tiniest bits of soil have captured and nurtured tiny seeds. The creek beds of southern Indiana give birth to geodes, those nondescript rocks that, when broken open, reveal breathtaking crystal formations. And diamonds—the most precious of gemstones—refract the colors of the spectrum as if they are alive with the energy of the universe.

This week, take time to contemplate Peter's image of you as a "living stone." Are you a gemstone or a geode? Granite or gypsum? What does it mean to be this "living stone" and how do you fit into Peter's "spiritual house" (another interesting metaphor to ponder another day)?

When you're out and about, keep your eyes open for the stones in your path. One of them is a metaphor for *you*! When you see it, bend over and pick it up. Put it in your pocket. Take it home. And put it in a place of honor where you will see it frequently to remind you that you are a vital "living stone" in the most important house ever created.

Gone Fishin'

Early in the morning, Jesus stood on the shore, but the disciples
did not realize that it was Jesus. He called out to them, "Friends,
haven't you any fish?" "No," they answered. He said, "Throw
your net on the right side of the boat and you will find some."
When they did, they were unable to haul the net in because of the
large number of fish. Then the disciple whom
Jesus loved said to Peter, "It is the Lord!"
John 21:4-7 NIV

I'm perched on my favorite rock in view of my husband, Rex, who stands hip deep
in the middle of the river. The sparkling water gurgles over the rocky riverbed,
framing a tiny, lone plant thriving on the slope of a rock settled midstream. It takes
so little earth in which a tiny seed may germinate! I've joined my husband here at
7:30 a.m., hoping to snag some inspiration for my writing. Tiny seedling ideas fall
upon the rocky ridges of my brain, but if I don't get them written down on paper,
they will not germinate.

I step gingerly into the brisk river, teetering among the mossy rocks. Splashing
water sings past me lustily, tugging playfully at my ankles. Investigating my hardy
little friend, I discover that she has found footing in a crevice of the rock, a
smattering of green moss keeping her company on the north face. I resettle
myself on a neighboring rock, and together, my little friend and I contemplate the
mysteries of life.

Poor Rex! The fish aren't biting, but a hungry log, eager for breakfast, takes the bait.
Rex abandons his fishing pole to go reclaim his wayward lure. Last night he lost a
brand, new bait on its maiden cast, the lifelike crawdad lodging stubbornly in a tree
branch hanging low over the bank. Today he's come prepared, intent on rescuing his
bait. A master problem solver, Rex has devised a rope and hook contraption that he
swings like a sling shot in the hopes of hooking his bait and pulling it from the crash
site. Just as he achieves enough momentum, the hook slaps the chest-high water and
sinks. His crafty plan is foiled.

Not easily discouraged, Rex heads for the riverbank, taking the dry path to the tree
in question. Lowering himself carefully down the steep bank into the shallows, he
again swings the rope and hook, this time achieving greater momentum and distance.
Alas, on each attempt the hook falls short of its prey. Mr. Crawdad, fine new bait
that he is, will enjoy life in the realm of his feathered contemporaries, never having
experienced the water world for which he was intended.

When I go fishing for words, I need to take inspiration from my fisher-husband who is amazingly patient with the slow and often frustrating process. Just as a portion of his fishing time is spent chasing after lost bait and untangling lines, I go in search of elusive descriptors and metaphors, suspended just out of reach in my cerebral branches, and struggle to untangle my thoughts and string them into words that will lure my readers in.

Writing requires a stubborn hope and faith that keeps the writer casting into the river of ideas flowing within. My internal waters are often shark-infested with powerful fears and insecurities that haunt the murky waters of self-revelation. Nevertheless, I must repeatedly lower myself down into the subterranean of my gray matter and raise my catch for all to see. The banks are steep, slippery and the depth unknowable. I must trust my instinct, the process, the Spirit to keep me afloat if I get in over my head. Am I willing to risk being seen? Sometimes, yes. Sometimes, no.

This sun-kissed morning reminds me of one of my favorite Bible passages: "Early in the morning, Jesus stood on the shore, but the disciples did not realize that it was Jesus. He called out to them, 'Friends, haven't you any fish?' 'No,' they answered. He said, 'Throw your net on the right side of the boat and you will find some.' When they did, they were unable to haul the net in because of the large number of fish." (John 21:4-6 NIV)

As I admire my husband's patience and persistence; as I marvel over the tenacious life clinging in the crevice of a river-bound rock; and as I contemplate bearing my soul to my readers, I am aware that Jesus is here with me, also. He guides my clumsy casts and fills my flimsy net. I haul up my catch and invite you to breakfast on the shore of my experience. Let's bow our heads together and say grace.

God of land and sea, when I lose my footing on the slippery rocks of life's uncertainties, and when my hopes and dreams dangle out of reach, help me to remember this grace-filled morning and its images of hope and persistence.

Close Encounters

We do not come to grace, grace comes to us. Try as we might to obtain grace, it may yet elude us. We may seek it not, yet it will find us. [13]
~ M. Scott Peck

*W*hen we first moved to our house, situated on a cliff overlooking the woods, I was itching to catch sight of the deer at play. Much to my dismay, my sightings are rare. It's probably because I always have Panda with me. While I walk quietly along a single path, Panda, the wonder dog, darts every which way, quite possibly covering in one excursion what I could barely manage to cover in a week. I'm sure she's easy for the deer to detect as she crashes through the brush, kicking up debris in hot pursuit of a fresh scent or a frisky squirrel.

One evening, as Rex and Panda and I were all enjoying the river, I had a much longed for close encounter. Rex was fishing just above the rapids, I was perched on a fallen tree, absorbing the sounds and fragrances of the woods and water, and Panda was wandering, checking in now and then to make sure I was okay. During one of her check-ins, her ears perked up as she sat quietly at my feet. Realizing that she was tracking the presence of another creature, I slowly leaned forward and took hold of her collar. If there was an animal close by, I didn't want her to frighten it away with an enthusiastic welcome.

Sure enough, I saw a deer—and then a second—out of the corner of my eye. Amazingly, there they were, off to my left, walking the levy path maybe thirty feet from where I sat. The summer foliage obscured my view, but sometimes a glimpse is much more exciting than a long look in full view. A glimpse keeps me hungering for more.

As the deer passed by, they looked our way, and then, stepping up their pace, disappeared into the camouflage of the woods. To my surprise, Panda sat picture-still, not moving a muscle as we observed our shy neighbors. If it had been a squirrel or raccoon, she would have yanked me off my perch and taken chase. It was almost as if we were sharing a spiritual experience with silence and reverence. In the spring, when the foliage is just

13 Peck, Scott, <u>The Road Less Traveled</u>, Simon & Schuster, 1978.

beginning to appear, and again in the fall, when it dies down, it's possible to occasionally detect the unobtrusive deer trails. During the summer, the trails become
virtually invisible, disappearing into the lush, green underbrush. In the winter, after
a snowfall, the presence of deer becomes magically displayed and it's possible to
follow the trails meandering through the thickest parts of the woods and skirting the
riverbank.

Dozens of trails crisscross the woods like a busy system of roads and highways,
lined tightly with an obstacle course of thickets, vines, and young saplings. How a
large antlered deer negotiates the terrain—and so quietly—I'll never know! As I
attempt to follow the fresh hoof prints, I feel like I'm in a video game, fighting off
thorns, stumbling over vines, tripping unceremoniously on fallen branches obscured
by the snow, and catching my hair in the web of branches overhead.

Rex and Panda returned from one of their winter excursions in the woods excitedly
reporting having followed a fresh trail. Panda nosed out the enticing scent in the
snow as Rex noted the crisp prints which suddenly changed from being closely and
evenly placed to being as much as eight feet apart. My hunters definitely had their
prey on the run. How frustrating to come so close and not even catch a glimpse of
the magnificent creature!

Sometimes God appears as elusive as the deer populating my woods. A spiritual
snowfall would be a great comfort to me, revealing evidence of God's path
intersecting my life in numerous yet unseen ways. Just a glimpse of God's footprints
in the snowfall of my wintry heart is all I ask for. I often trudge through the woods,
lost in thought, oblivious to the signs around me of the deer who graze along my
path. Similarly, I probably miss evidence of God because my eyes are glazed over,
my mind deep in reflection, or maybe I'm even complaining silently in prayer about
God's seeming truancy in my life.

I cringe to think of all the times I've missed a close encounter with God! When a
friend says to me, "I waved at you yesterday, but you didn't see me," I'm always
disappointed that I missed the opportunity to connect. And I am sad when I'm the
one doing the waving, and my friend fails to smile and say "Hi!" If on that particular
day I'm also feeling depressed, lonely, or sad, I might even find myself worrying that
my friend was purposely ignoring or snubbing me. I wonder how God feels when I
don't smile and wave back…

My precious glimpses of deer—and grace—restore my vigilance and hope for future
sightings. Peering deeply into the dense foliage, a maze of green in constant motion,
I try to will a deer or God into my line of sight. Of course, this doesn't work and I
must relax and practice a state of attentiveness, an openness to and readiness for an
unannounced, impossible-to-predict *crosspoint* with Grace.

Playing Possum

Why do you look for the living among the dead?
He is not here; he has risen!
Luke 24:5-6 NIV

A couple of weeks ago, Panda and I took my good friend, Zola, for a walk in the wintry woods. As is her custom, Panda dashed on ahead of us enjoying her frolic in the snow. As my friend and I caught up with Panda, I noticed that she had something in her mouth. "Panda, put that down!" I shouted, and surprisingly, she did, but continued to stand guard over her treasure. Curled up at her feet was a possum, looking dead as a doornail. Naively, I stooped over and picked up the lifeless possum. Like Panda, my curiosity gets the best of me sometimes.

After a quick look, I placed the limp possum back on the ground and continued to look at it. "He's not dead," Zola declared, amused at my ignorance. "He's playing possum!" Duh! As you can imagine, I felt pretty dumb. Of course he was playing possum! That's what possums are famous for. It did seem like his mouth twitched just a little, but it wasn't until we stopped to look for him, on our return trip, that there was proof positive he was faking it: he was gone!

Later that evening, when I told Rex about our encounter in the woods, he reminded me, "You don't pick up possums! Possums are nasty! Possums carry rabies!" Usually I'm the one warning and cautioning Rex for what I consider to be reckless brushes with wildlife (he can't resist picking up snakes). But this time, I was on the receiving end, and appropriately so.

I'm going to make a b-i-g leap here, so hang on tight! On Easter Sunday—the first Easter Sunday, so many years ago—Jesus' beloved friends went to his tomb early in the morning—and like my possum, Jesus was gone! Unlike this wily creature, though, Jesus wasn't playing possum. How could this be! They had witnessed his death with their own eyes and seen to it that his body had been laid to rest in a tomb. Imagine their confusion and panic as they struggled to make sense of what made no sense to the human mind.

You may be standing on the far side of the creek, a puzzled look on your face, wondering how on earth I've leapt into an analogy between our Risen Savior and—of all things—an ugly, rat-like creature. Bear with me for a moment. Many skeptics of Jesus' day, and throughout the centuries, have doubted Jesus' resurrection. "Oh, that's just a story," they say. Or, perhaps, while believing that Jesus was a real historical person, they might, however, argue, "but his resurrection is just a myth." Might some among those skeptics also have said, "He was just 'playing possum'"? There must have been dozens of outlandish theories and rumors about what really happened.

Silly as it may seem to you, from now on, when I see a possum, I will be reminded of the resurrection and the gifts of salvation and life everlasting. This is one of the ways God speaks to me and captures my attention. Be on the alert for how God is reaching out to you—and take a leap into the passion and resurrection that leads to life eternal.

Glimpses of Grace

Now we see but a poor reflection as in a mirror; then we shall see
face to face. Now I know in part; then I shall know fully,
even as I am fully known.

1 Corinthians 13:12 NIV

I just love the way God grabs my attention when I am lost in thought. He gives me glimpses of grace that provide new perspectives on life—captured in a blink of the eye, out of the corner of the eye.

Following one of my many walks in the woods, I noticed that the right lens of my glasses seemed dirty. I get really perturbed that my lenses always seem to be smudged and speckled, but my irritability transformed to amazed delight as I scrutinized my lens. Delicately plastered on the outside of the glass was a perfectly preserved portion of a spider web. I couldn't believe that I had walked around for several hours, looking right through the web, never noticing it!

Obviously I had walked into a web that had been dangling over the path and "caught" the web instead of it capturing me. A few years ago I would have yelped "YUK!" and been freaked out at the possibility that I'd also carried home an eight-legged creepy-crawler nesting in my hair as well. Instead, I reacted by laughing, engaging those cute little crinkles that have only recently begun to form around my eyes and mouth. I felt like God was throwing back his head and laughing boisterously with me, delighted that I'd finally discovered his sneaky little gift.

God knows that I've never been fond of spiders. Even reading Charlotte's Web with my children, while reducing me to tears with Wilbur when dear Charlotte died, has not been able to crack through my abhorrence for arachnids. I just can't seem to cleanse my mind of that big hairy, bug spray-defying spider that lived with Rex and me when we first moved to Anderson and set up housekeeping in an adorable town house apartment. Our Charlotte loved to slip out of the crack between the outside wall of the living room and the foundation and peer at me, flaunting her superiority, knowing full well that I wouldn't come within ten feet of her. Imagine her surprise when I armed myself with bug spray, charged at her, and misted her with bullets of poison. Imagine my surprise when she "took her licking and kept on ticking!" God's creatures are feisty and resilient!

Just a few weeks before I wore that spider web home on my glasses, God gave me an incredible glimpse of grace into the beauty of the world of spiders, setting the scene for me to welcome my upcoming web-entanglement with humor. Prior to going to bed one evening, Rex had put Panda and Trixie outside and had spotted a web in progress framed in a window in our sun room, brilliantly illuminated by the rays of the porch light. Knowing of my love of nature, Rex coaxed me to come take a look.

"Isn't it just like God to take on the challenge of capturing our attention out of the corner of our eyes..."

I stood spellbound for the next thirty minutes, caught up in wonder and appreciation for the love God has for his creation, demonstrated in and for even the tiniest of his creatures. Unaware of my presence and oblivious to being in the spotlight, Charlotte went about her business with skill and confidence, weaving a breathtaking architectural wonder. Spinning deftly, her creation swayed delicately, its filigree of fibers sparkling in the light, as each appendage cooperated in an intricately choreographed dance encoded eons ago by the Master Creator.

Isn't it just like God to take on the challenge of capturing our attention out of the corner of our eyes, drawing us into a new understanding and appreciation of that which we don't understand or appreciate? While we dash headlong—or drag ourselves—into our day, the miracle of God's love lavishly displayed right in front of our noses (and eyes), we often miss the sunrise of God's love, the whisper of the Spirit in the soft breeze, the sparkle in Christ's eyes reflected in an impish child or playful pup, the myriad of extraordinary ways that God's presence and grace are woven and spun into the very fibers of our lives.

While I'm still not fond of spiders, God has used my arachnid encounters to help me look beyond my negative reactions for glimpses of grace in even the worst of circumstances. What in your life is God calling you to take a fresh look at out of the corner of your eye?

The Hunter

"You will seek me and find me when you seek me with all your heart."
Jeremiah 29:13 NIV

"*W*ould you like to hear a funny story?" Rex said, a twinkle in his eye. He was stretched out comfortably on the floor in front of the TV and I was sitting on the sofa behind him. He lit up with a big smile, eager to share a bright spot of his day with me.

"Sure!" I said, smiling back.

"Do you remember me telling you about the hunter I saw about a month ago who was using a life-size decoy of a deer?" Rex and Panda had been out for a walk in the woods and as they approached a clearing, Rex spotted a deer. The deer turned out to be a decoy, the hunter stationed up the hill from them, sitting on a large rock. Panda, the scaredy-cat of our canine family, would not go near the decoy. She's not afraid to chase a squirrel, corner a feisty raccoon on the deck, or pick up a possum who's "playin' possum," but a plastic deer is w-a-y out of her comfort zone. Rex had a dickens of a time getting her to cross the field that she usually bounds across in several joyous leaps. You can never be too cautious around a plastic deer!

"Well, today I had a hunter in the office and we got to talking about hunting. I asked him if he'd ever used a decoy." "I did once," he replied. Remembering the decoy he had recently seen, Rex inquired, "Where were you hunting at the time?" It turns out that he was the very hunter—and very same decoy—that Rex had seen. What a coincidence! He told Rex that he had been quite amused by Panda's unnecessarily cautious reaction to his decoy.

"What's *really* funny," the hunter added, "is that the very next day I was hunting in the same spot, without the decoy, when you wife and daughter walked by." He had surmised who we were because Panda was with us. "I was actually watching a deer and they were totally oblivious." Panda, too, was clueless. The deer, however, watched the three unobservant intruders ambling along and did not so much as switch its tail. Obviously, it was quite apparent that we were no threat to him. Fortunately for the deer, he was out of range for the hunter.

I laughed heartily at this story in which I was one of the comical characters. I remembered well the day Beth, Panda, and I took this walk, a few days before Christmas. I had noted the hunter hunched, still as a statue, on the rock. Each time I spot a hunter, I experience an immediate jolt of adrenaline. It's a little unnerving to realize that, unbeknownst to me, I'm being watched by someone with a shotgun or high powered bow. During hunting season, Panda sports a bright orange bandanna, a "red flag" to hunters that her fawn-colored coat and white backside and undertail do not spell "d-e-e-r." I've looked for the hunter since, every time I cross that meadow, but he's not been there. While I do not "get" hunting, I understand that it is legal, and I don't want to ruin anyone else's enjoyment of the woods. When Panda and I trudge through, noisily disrupting a hunter's territory, I feel a bit guilty. I imagine that he's been sitting on that hard rock, frost nipping at his nose, for hours, patiently waiting for a deer to appear, and then we crash through, probably ruining his chances of even seeing a deer, let alone taking it home to his freezer. If it were me (hunting with a camera, of course), I would be bored to tears with the laborious wait and then frustrated and furious with whomever it was that ruined my hunt. For the most part, however, I am relieved that my presence may have saved a deer a trip to a dinner table.

> "How many times, I wonder, have I been the object of a deer's curiosity?"

I complain and complain about never seeing deer in the woods, blaming it on the fact that Panda is always with me, racing ahead, boisterously announcing our presence. Now I know that, truth be told, I'm just not very observant. I can't help but appreciate the humor in knowing that I am being watched by the very creature that I so long to see. How many times, I wonder, have I been the object of a deer's curiosity? I certainly hope he enjoys a glimpse of me as much as I would of him. I'd like to think that one of us has thrilled at the sight of another of God's amazing creatures.

There's a metaphor here of my relationship with God. How many times, I wonder, have I passed within a hair's breath of God, oblivious—and mistakenly disappointed that God did not show up. My "missing" God is never about God not showing up. It is about my lack of vision. What is it that Jesus said about having eyes to see and ears to hear?

There's a lot I could learn from that hunter perched patiently and perceptively on a rock…

Chapter II

Seeds, Weeds, and Needs: Growing In Grace

Whether you tend a garden or not,
you are the gardener of your own being,
the seed of your destiny.
~ *The Findhorn Community*[14]

What is a weed?
A plant whose virtues
have not yet been discovered.
~ *Ralph Waldo Emerson*

Pussy Willows

I love my pussy willow bush
when the pussy willows come out.
It's one of the first signs of spring
without the slightest doubt.

They look like little kittens
as they snuggle close together,
in order to stay warm
if there's a change in weather.

Sometimes I stand and listen,
pretend I hear them purr.
I know that's impossible--
wouldn't it be nice, if they were?
~ *Marjorie Reuman Rettke*[15]

---

14 The Findhorn Community, <u>The Findhorn Garden</u>, Perennial (Harper Collins), November 1976.
15 "Pussy Willows" was written by my aunt. When my children were young, Aunt Marge would send
   them poems, some of which were written especially for them. Aunt Marge and I shared a passion for
   nature and God's creatures—a proclivity we inherited from her father, Reuben Reuman.

❧ The Mustard Seed

The kingdom of heaven is like a mustard seed, which a man took and planted in his field. Though it is the smallest of all your seeds, yet when it grows, it is the largest of garden plants and becomes a tree, so that the birds of the air come and perch in its branches.
Matthew 13:31-32 NIV

Many years ago, this little parable was planted in my soul by my mother. As a small child, I used to worry that my faith was not "big" or "good" enough to get me into heaven, "…if I should die before I wake." During my moments of spiritual angst, Mom would tell me the story of the mustard seed and assure me that my tiny seed of faith was enough, and that it would eventually bush out. At one point she even gave me a mustard seed necklace (a pendant consisting of a small, clear, bead containing a mustard seed)—the '50's equivalent of today's "WWJD" bracelets—to remind me of the miracle of faith.

> "Through the years, a variety of special people have tended my little seed and it did indeed bush out."

Through the years, a variety of special people have tended my little seed and it did indeed bush out. I am blessed by the image of the branches of my faith providing shade for others who perch for awhile in my life. And I am thankful for the opportunity to sit in the shade of the faith of other believers. Whether your faith is seed or bush, it is enough.

"…if you have faith as small as a mustard seed, you can say to this mountain, 'Move from here to there' and it will move. Nothing will be impossible for you."
Matthew 17:20

Seasons of the Soil

Based on the Parable of the Sower
Matthew 13:1-9, 18-23 NIV

*T*here's nothing quite as satisfying as pulling weeds. I love to pull up all the "squatters" who have laid claim to my flower beds, and then stand back and admire my work. It gives me great satisfaction and pleasure. Perhaps you are thinking "Linda, get a life!" Please, read on.

Every spring I clear out the forest of miniature maple trees that appears every year about this time. I look at those cute little trees, appreciating their darling little leaves, and then with mild regret, grab them by their delicate stems and pull them gently from the earth. I can feel their tenacious fingerling roots giving way against my brute strength. If I hadn't come along and disturbed their growth, I wonder how many of those seedlings would grow into towering, shade-giving maple trees like the one in my backyard from which they fell.

This brings me to my point: according to Jesus, God's Word is like a seed falling on the ground, just like those helicopters that whirl and spin, falling into my flower bed. Is my heart like the hard path where the seed falls, fails to root, and is eaten by a bird? Is your heart similar to the rocks where there wasn't much soil, such that the seed quickly shoots forth a plant that quickly withers in the sun for lack of firm roots? Are our hearts thorny, choking God's word before it has a chance to "leaf out," or are we like the rich soil from which bounty springs?

I'm inclined to believe that the soil of my heart varies from season to season, depending on the "weather conditions" in my life. My heart's desire is to be like the dark, rich loam found on Grandma and Grandpa Baumerts' farm in northern Indiana. But even when I'm not, I know that God will still cultivate me, fertilize me, weed out my rocks, ward off the insects, bless me with sunshine and rain, give me seasons of rest beneath a blanket of snow—and most importantly, show up again next spring to plant more seeds.

Spaciousness [16]

Grow in the grace and knowledge of our Lord and Savior Jesus Christ.
2 Peter 3:18 NIV

*L*ately the words space, spacious, and spaciousness have been leaping off the pages of everything I've been reading. Thinking perhaps that God is speaking to me, I've become more observant of the spaces around me.

One spring day as I was driving in the country, I noticed the cornfields stretching in every direction. Suddenly I became aware of the spaces between the long, even rows of green shoots. I remember as a novice gardener tediously spacing seeds in my vegetable patch, according to package directions. I thought it was such a waste to leave so much space between those tiny seeds.

I think the message of the Master Gardener is this: in order for me to grow spiritually and emotionally, I need to give myself space. I tend to fill up the spaces of my life with all sorts of worthy and not-so-worthy activities. My busy calendar reflects my deeper purpose of attempting to fill up the emptiness and incompleteness I feel inside.

Slowly God has shifted my focus from the produce of my life to the empty spaces within. I've discovered that my incompleteness and emptiness serve as fertile ground where I can encounter God's love and grace.

How are you crowding out God's love and grace? What can you do today to meet God in your emptiness?

---

16 Teeple, Linda, "Spaciousness," <u>Voices of Hope: Daily Meditations for Persons In Recovery,</u> Caroline Smith, Ed., Warner Press.

Our Eternal Farmer

Further Thoughts on the Parable of the Sower
Matthew 13:1-9, 18-23

My soul is a poor land, plenteous in dearth—
Here blades of grass, there a small herb for food—
A nothing that would be something if it could.
~ George MacDonald [17]

*Y*ears ago, my friend, Carol, introduced me to the nineteenth century author, George MacDonald. Together, we read our way through numerous MacDonald novels, enjoying the wonderful stories and the truths of God's grace woven through the stories like a fine, gold thread. So it was with delight that I came across the above quote while reading a book on parables.

In the Parable of the Sower, Jesus likens our souls to soil. Sometimes the soil of our souls is like a hard-packed path, unable to receive the seed of God's word. For whatever reason, we are unable or unwilling to listen. At other times, our souls respond to God's voice like a rocky path, initially responding with enthusiasm and allowing His word to take hold in the crevices amid the rocks. But, alas, our enthusiasm is short-lived. And then there are those times when our souls are infiltrated with thorns that choke out our awareness of and reliance on God's grace.

To complicate matters, the thorns that capture our attention aren't always bad. Like the thorns of a rose, we have many wonderful blessings—beautiful homes and possessions, stimulating and demanding jobs, priceless relationships—that are cause for worry, **"We dare not give up on anyone."** consuming our time and energy and drawing our attention away from the Eternal. Unlike the hard-packed and rocky times of our souls, thorns appear when our souls are often the most hospitable and capable of great productivity, but our attention is on things other than cultivating spiritual seeds.

Given the shifting seasons of our souls, it is a miracle that anything can take root and grow! I'm sure we can all identify with MacDonald's lament that his soul is "a poor land" and "a nothing that would be something if it could." However, J. Ellsworth Kalas, states that "Whenever we serve as witnesses to the faith, we must do so with all earnestness, because one doesn't know the season in which the soul currently abides. That uninterested, distracted, or unresponsive person may be nearer the Kingdom than we—or they—realize. The truth of it is, we dare not give up on anyone at any time—including ourselves."[18]

17 MacDonald, George, Diary of an Old Soul, A.C. Fifield, 1905.
18 Kalas, J. Ellsworth, Parables from the Back Side: Bible Stories with a Twist, Abingdon Press, 1992, p. 40. Used by permission.

On the way home from church one Sunday, Rex told me an amazing fact that he'd heard on TV. Seeds found in an ancient tomb, estimated to be five thousand years old, actually grew when planted! Five thousand years old! All that was needed was a little water and nurturing. As Kalas says, "We dare not give up on anyone."

With our Eternal Farmer in charge, anything is possible!

The one who received the seed that fell on good soil is the man
who hears the word and understands it. He produces a crop,
yielding a hundred, sixty or thirty times what was sown.
Matthew 13:23 NIV

Why should I tremble at the plough of my Lord,
that maketh deep furrows on my soul?
I know He is no idle husbandman,
he purposeth a crop.
~ Samuel Rutherford[19]

---

19 Samuel Rutherford (1600-1661), English minister and author, published a book in 1636 defending the doctrines of grace, setting him at odds with Church authorities. This resulted in his being stripped of his ministerial office and being exiled to Scotland.

Chapter III

Blossoms and Bugs: The Garden of Grace

To see a World in a Grain of Sand
And a heaven in a Wild Flower,
Hold infinity in the palm of your hand
And Eternity in an hour.
~ William Blake

"Hope" is the thing with feathers –
That perches in the soul –
And sings the tune without the words –
And never stops – at all –
And sweetest – in the Gale – is heard –
And sore must be the storm –
That could abash the little Bird
That kept so many warm –
I've heard it in the chillest land –
And on the strangest Sea –
Yet, never, in Extremity,
It asked a crumb – of Me.
~ Emily Dickinson

Bugs.
Bugs drive me crazy.
I was crazy once.
They locked me up in a padded room
and threw away the key…
Bugs.
Bugs drive me crazy…
(repeat endlessly)[20]

---

20 My children loved to torment me endlessly with this annoying little ditty.

Hope Springs Eternal

May the God of hope fill you with all joy and peace as you trust in him,
so that you may overflow with hope by the power of the Holy Spirit.
Romans 15:13 NIV

*E*very few years I purchase a hanging fuchsia plant, bursting with excitement as I eagerly await the blossoming of the abundant, vibrant, delicate buds. We start out great, my fuchsia and I, content in each other's adoring attention. About three weeks into our relationship, our attentiveness starts to lag. I forget to water it; it stops producing blooms. I over-water it; its leaves turn yellow and drop off. I don't ever actually give up on the plant entirely, but looking at its sparse leaves and nonexistent flowers induces guilt for my neglect, which saps all the fun out of my care-giving.

 Last fall, I decided to bring my pathetic fuchsia inside and see if I could nurture it back to life. By the time I trimmed off all the dead foliage, there were precious few spindly stems bearing precious few tiny, sickly leaves. Every so often, I would trim it back a little in the hopes of it bushing out. It barely grew—but it didn't die, so I kept watering it.

When summer came, I took my struggling fuchsia outside and hung it on a shepherd's hook on my deck railing. I was concerned that this location would provide too much sun, but since it didn't thrive in its previous more shady location, I decided to see what would happen. There was certainly nothing to lose. I watered; it didn't die. I watered; it grew a wee, tiny bit. And then, just a week ago, it surprised me with its first bud in over a year. I was elated! Now the buds are coming fast and furious, displaying lovely fuchsia and purple blossoms. What joy to see the fruits of our labor and persistence—and *hope*! While it's not the enormous, lush plant that I purchased a year ago, it is definitely a living testimony to the miracle of TLC.

> "If such miracles are possible in nature, this has also got to be true in personal relationships as well."

My precious little fuchsia is proof-positive that "hope springs eternal." If such miracles are possible in nature, this has also got to be true in personal relationships as well. Sometimes I'm the lush plant, bursting with potential. At other times, I'm the hopeful yet less than perfect gardener whose dedication waxes and wanes. Our relationships with each other—including our relationships with God—wax and wane and are in need of our constant attention.

As a therapist, I far too often see relationships dying on the vine. A well-meaning husband neglects the emotional needs of his wife and children, caught up in his career. A wife repeatedly criticizes her spouse, unknowingly eroding his self-esteem and commitment to his marriage. Entangled in the weeds of bitterness, stubbornness, and hurt, couples lose the ability to listen to, encourage, and support each other.

Unfortunately, many individuals, couples, and families arrive at my office declaring counseling to be a last ditch effort at fixing their strained relationships. The hard set of a jaw, the hurt visible in tear-filled eyes, and the presence of protective, rigid walls tell me that I have my work cut out for me. If they stick with me (often their minds are made up before they even set foot in my office), I will gather my watering can, clippers, fertilizer, and weed killer and get to work.

What keeps me weeding in this garden—both that of my own relationships, and the weedy gardens of my clients? Hope. Hope *and* confidence that the Holy Spirit is diligently at work in our tender, fragile relationships. Abuse, neglect, infidelity, divorce, and other crises of relationships are realities in the garden of life, but nevertheless, my hope springs eternal. What joy I feel when, like my struggling fuchsia, my own relationships and those of others spring back to life, stronger and more beautiful than before—a living testament to God's healing love and grace.

Hope springs eternal!

But those who hope in the Lord will renew their strength.
They will soar on wings like eagles;
they will run and not grow weary,
they will walk and not be faint.
Isaiah 40:31 NIV

Mosquitoes

*C*an anyone tell me the purpose of a mosquito? Does this aggravation have any redeeming value? What was Noah *thinking* when he invited a pesky pair for a sail?

Mosquitoes cause diseases like malaria, yellow fever, encephalitis, and West Nile Virus. They also induce annoying itching and scratching, and, this summer in particular, they've managed to make it impossible to enjoy being outside for more than a nanosecond. Not-to-be-outwitted-Rex has been ever vigilant spraying and fogging the yard with every product on the market invented for the eradication, or at least, containment, of the population explosion of mosquitoes, in the hopes that we could venture outdoors. Instead, we've been held hostage in our own home, where we wistfully gaze out the window upon a summer swiftly waning away. I've been praying for cold weather—something I don't think I've ever done before!

"Why on earth," you ask, "did you pick the mosquito to ponder?" I don't think I did the picking. *It* picked me. The nasty nip of a mosquito-in-residence serves as my inspiration.

What actually cinched the deal to write about this bitter, biting scourge-of-summer is that, earlier this week, I recommended the video, "How To Win At Parenting Without Beating Your Kids," to a parent who is in counseling with me. I recommend this video a lot! In the introduction, the speaker, Barbara Coloroso, invites her audience to "irritate" (see the connection: mosquito—irritate?) on her creative strategies meant to inspire better parenting. She "stings" her listeners with her wit and wisdom, leaving them mentally scratching long after they leave the auditorium.

Well, that certainly helps put the mosquito into a more positive light—if only *metaphorically*! Perhaps my "pondering" is a variation on "irritating." An idea gets under my skin, I scratch at it for awhile, and it welts up and turns red. (Hmm… this metaphor isn't quite working) …I scratch at it for awhile and an idea begins to itch its way to the surface where it irritates me until I transfer it to paper or floppy disk. "Pondering" conjures up a much more pleasing image than "irritating," does it not? I ponder appealing, intriguing ideas, but when I irritate, I'm struggling with challenging, unsettling ideas. "Irritating" pushes and shoves me out of my comfort zone.

I associate "pondering" with Mary, the mother of Jesus, who "treasured up all these things and pondered them in her heart" (Luke 2:19 NIV). Jesus, on the other hand, caused his listeners to "irritate," especially the religious leaders. Putting a new spin on things with his inspiring sermons and puzzling parables, Jesus managed to *really* bug the holier-than-thous. Christ's "spin," of course, was the message of Grace. Under the umbrella of grace, Christ violated the Judaic law by healing the sick on the Sabbath. Jesus' choice of friends really got under the skin of the religious leaders, too, just as an adolescent's choice of friends irritates the daylights out of concerned parents. He hung out with the wrong crowd all right: sinners, like prostitutes, tax collectors, and Samaritans; and the less fortunate, like lepers, the lame and blind, the poor. And to top it all off, he wasn't afraid to call a spade a spade—or a Pharisee a hypocrite![21]

I much prefer to picture Grace as an elegant, delicate, *miraculous* butterfly, gracefully fluttering among the flowers. I gasp in awe at her beauty and pause, spellbound, in her gracious presence. Perhaps God uses both the butterfly and the mosquito to draw us into "the grace that passes all understanding." I'm going to have to "irritate" on this for awhile…

…*and*, I think I'll keep the hydrocortisone cream handy!

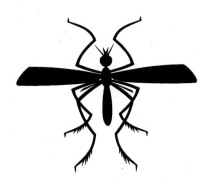

---

21 To" read more about it," check out the "Seven Woes" in Matthew 23.

# Late Bloomer

"For I know the plans I have for you," declared the Lord,
"plans to prosper you and not to harm you, plans to
give you hope and a future."
Jeremiah 29:11 NIV

Sitting on my deck one day, golden, crisp leaves drifting down gently around me from the tulip tree towering over me, I happen to glance up from my reading and gaze off in the distance, lost in thought. Unbeknownst to me, my focus shifts away from my inner thoughts, and I suddenly notice something quite peculiar.

> "Like my flowering crab tree, sometimes I defy the odds and bloom when least expected"

A few feet from my deck stands a flowering crab tree which is a spectacular sight in the spring, so full of beautiful, fragrant, pink blossoms that it looks like a soft, pink cloud. This past spring had not been a good one for this normally robust tree. Speckled with a few meager blossoms, it lagged into summer with a leafing that seemed tired and sparse. As the summer progressed, the tree has looked more and more distressed, perhaps from the heat and dryness of late summer. I've wondered if its years of prolific blooming has worn it out.

On this early fall afternoon, this sad looking tree catches my attention, willing me to notice that it is blooming—blooming in the middle of September, following a long, dry spell that has left large patches of my lawn dying in ground that is beginning to crack open. Blooming in spite of the fact that my annuals and perennials are limp and lifeless because my enthusiasm for gardening has waned with the heat and mosquitoes. While the hose lays useless, the flowering crab defies nature and blooms. Granted, its not the spectacular display of spring, but its a grand effort at a time when everything else is tired—including the tree itself.

I can't help but think about how I, too, am a late bloomer. Solidly planted in middle age, the promise of AARP discounts on the horizon, I find myself blooming in unique ways, in spite of the fact that my springs aren't as glorious and my branches not as sturdy and leafy. Like my flowering crab tree, sometimes I defy the odds and bloom when least expected. How comforting it is to know that there are exceptions to the laws of nature, *and* exceptions to the laws of *human* nature.

So my tree and middle-aged me invite you to bloom when you least expect it, where you least expect it, in ways you least expect.

Toadal Frustration

(With sincere apologies to Mr. Toad, from the gardener)

I'm not much of a gardener—mainly I'm a get-excited-in-the-spring; abandon-the-garden-in-the dog-days-of-summer kind of gardener. Like the spring rains, I nurture my flowers, watering frequently, weeding, cutting off the dead flowers, weeding, watering. And like the heat of August, I quickly fizzle when I sizzle, retreating to the comfort of my air conditioned house where I relax, sipping a cold glass of raspberry ice tea.

It's mid September and I'm proud to say that I'm still making an effort to tend my precious babies, although this dry spell is testing my devotion. My routine involves spraying myself thoroughly with bug repellent and throwing myself to the mosquitoes who are not to be fooled by a little chemical barrier and are soon attracted to my sweat as it swiftly washes off the repellent. I fill up my watering cans and lug them to the front yard where I give each flower a generous drink of water. I know that there is an easier way to accomplish the task, but I continue to fill, lug, and quench. I love to be outdoors, so I don't care that I'm not being time-efficient.

"Life in the watering can can be a tumultuous wash, can it not?"

One afternoon, I noticed something floating in one of my watering cans. Thinking that it was a leaf, I ignored it and kept to my task. After I was done, I placed the can back in its rightful spot by the hose caddie—and noticed a scratching sound coming from the can. Low and behold, what I thought was a leaf was actually a toad!

Just imagine what Mr. Toad's tenure in the can must have been like! There he is, minding his own business, quietly contemplating toadly concerns, when all of a sudden, he finds himself in a deluge of water riveting down on him from my highly specialized nozzle which, by the way, I have set on "jet." Up he floats, as the water rises, to the top of the can, finding himself smooshed between the can and the churning water surface, precious little breathing room to boot. Much to his relief, the water level begins to drop, eventually depositing him safely on the bottom of the can once again.

Oh, oh! Look out below!

Water once again pellets him, and slowly floats him to the top amid the roiling waters. And the cycle repeats itself again and again. *Finally*, the can is dropped to the ground where it tips over, allowing an escape. While toads can hop quickly, avoiding capture, they can also be tentative in their actions. Mr. Toad takes his time, resting cautiously on the threshold. He listens patiently as I offer my condolences and apologies for the traumatic experience I have caused him to endure.

As I continue my yard work, I peek back occasionally, to see if Mr. Toad is still debating whether to stay or flee. Yes, He's still debating… and debating… and debating… and finally I look and the watering can threshold is toadless. But he's not ventured far. I can see him hiding out in the shade under the heat pump.

I've had days like this, haven't you? Life in the watering can can be a tumultuous wash, can it not? Such days you just want to say, "Can it!" and go back to bed. I could go on and on with my canny humor, but I won't. Gotta' go water my flowers! But before I do, I'd like to share with you David's words of blessing for difficult days:

May the Lord answer you when you are in distress;
May the name of the God of Jacob protect you.
May he send you help from the sanctuary and grant you support from Zion.
Psalm 20:1-2 NIV

The Grape Vine

I am the true vine, and my Father is the gardener,
...you are the branches.
John 15:1,5 NIV

*O*n a hot, summer day, a little girl lies sprawled out beneath the foliage of a grape vine. Shaded by the dense, leafy growth, she breathes in the tantalizing aroma of the ripening fruit. Gazing upward through the vines, humming a tune and talking softly to herself, she views the immense blue sky and is warmed by the sun's intense rays that find their way through the arbor to her already sun-browned skin. In her own private Garden of Eden, she is at peace with her Creator.

I am that little girl—or at least I was, many years ago. One of the treasures of my childhood home was a large backyard, bordered on one side by a grape arbor yielding purple, green *and* red grapes. I loved to lounge under the vines and look at the sky, eating from the luscious fruit of the vine. I was in heaven and, in those moments, all was right with my world.

So it is with delicious childhood memories that I contemplate the spiritual metaphor in which Jesus, the vine, his Father, the gardener, and I, are entangled.

Jesus tells us,

> *"Remain in me, and I will remain in you. No branch can bear fruit by itself; it must remain in the vine. Neither can you bear fruit unless you remain in me. I am the vine; you are the branches. If a man remains in me and I in him, he will bear much fruit; apart from me you can do nothing" (John 15:4-5 NIV).*

How I want to be like the grapevine of my childhood, yielding juicy, plump, fragrant clusters of life-sustaining, delicious fruit!

I picture my life in its entirety as a full cluster of grapes, with the many things I think and do in life as the individual grapes. My "best of show" fruit consists of many tiny acts of love, self-discipline, obedience, sacrifice, and creativity. While much of my fruit is juicy and tasty, there are more than a few "sour grapes" and wizened fruit mixed in—signs of my blemished record, rotten attitudes, and bitter words.

This metaphor naturally brings to mind the fruit of the Spirit: love, joy, peace, patience, kindness, goodness, faithfulness, gentleness and self control (Galatians 5: 22-23). God keeps constant vigil in the vineyard of my life, pruning, weeding, watering, and fertilizing, to cultivate the fruit of the Spirit within me.

There's some major pruning going on right now. My life is cluttered with distractions and "things—lots of things" that draw my attention away from God. My daughter, Beth, shared with me a fascinating book that consists of photographs taken of people and all their worldly possessions. People from all walks of life, and from dozens of different countries, are pictured standing in front of their dwellings, surrounded by everything they own. In the pictures of the humblest of third world homes, the viewer is struck by the material lack, which stands out in stark contrast to the middle class American yards piled high with a profusion of possessions.

I would be embarrassed and ashamed to have my pack-rat greed exposed in such a graphic way! As a book-a-holic, I could easily start my own library. When I occasionally prune my collection, my husband, Rex, hauls my cast offs to the library, where he jokes with the librarian that they will need to reinforce the floor to handle the weight of my contribution to the Friends of the Library. Then there's my clothes, photo albums, angel collection, Christmas decorations… (Well, you get the picture!)

God is in my attic, sifting through my stash of past hurts, regrets, and other unnecessary what-nots that I just can't seem to part with. Who knows what's buried in the basement that he hasn't gotten to yet! How on earth there's time on God's docket to prune all the rest of you, I'll never know! Fortunately, God is passionate about the fruit of his vine and labors tirelessly to improve its quality and yield.

The vinedresser is never nearer the branches
then when he is pruning them.
~ David Jeremiah[22]

God may be in the process of pruning something out of
your live at this very moment. If this is the case, don't
fight it. Instead, welcome it, for His pruning will make you
more fruitful and bring greater glory to the Father.
~ Rick Yohn[23]

---

22 Dr. David Jeremiah is the senior pastor of Shadow Mountain Community Church in El Cajon, California, author of many books, and the host of "Turning Point," a radio ministry that is heard around the world.

23 Rick Yohn is the pastor of Fellowship Community Church in Centennial, Colorado and the author of numerous books and Bible studies.

Bug-Light

He spoke, and there came swarms of flies, and gnats...
Psalm 105:31 NIV

*A*h, nature! While I'm partial to furry, fuzzy, cuddly critters, occasionally my attention is taken captive outside the woolly realm of mammalian warmth:

During the heat of summer, I relish the opportunity to light the Tiki torches on the mossy-bricked patio, where our domestic domicile meets the wooded cliff, and curl up on my swing to read in the pleasant coolness of the evening. As my eyes scan the pages illuminated by my tiny book light, my mind absorbed in images and ideas, the pungency of citronella stinging my nostrils, my senses are double-tasking, on the alert for a snap of a twig or a wiggle of leaves in the absence of a breeze, signs that a four-footed visitor may be cautiously approaching. An eerie "whoo-o-o-o-o" mingles with a whispered whistle of an approaching train, the drone of a single-engine sand-piper taking flight from the nearby airstrip, and the chorus of cheers from the parent-infested bleachers surrounding a ball diamond on the far side of the river.

Despite the citronella oil, and its renowned reputation for warding off insects, bugs are beckoned by the irresistible gravitational pull of my battery-powered, high-intensity light rays. The literary leaves now function as a landing strip for all sorts of bugs wooed and enamored by the light. My longing for enlightenment is compromised by my winged friends' hunger for light. Who's to say that *my* needs are more important than those of the bugs! Granted, books are created to impart knowledge and provide entertainment, but I delight in the creativity and ingenuity of the tiny critters sunbathing on the beaches of wisdom. My environmentalist-within relishes and welcomes the opportunity for my light to serve a dual purpose.

Absorbed in a book about grace, nothing was further from my mind than investigating bugs. Nevertheless, after brushing away a truly amazing array of "pests," my focus begrudgingly shifted to this tinker-bell ballet—a command performance staged under the floodlights of Grace—for this hand-picked audience of one. In spite of my irritation with this seeming interruption, I had to laugh. Was God trying to get my attention? What was I missing?

Always intrigued and amazed by God's infinite and outrageous creativity, in this particular moment of grace, I marveled in the sampling of bugs sharing my light. I was especially captured by how tiny some of the bugs were and wished that I had a magnifying glass at my ready to get a closer look. And where do all these bugs come from? Do they live here in my yard, right under my nose, yet invisible, undetected? (Or is it *I* who is crashing the party in *their* yard?)

Why on earth does God need so many different kinds of bugs? It must be that God has the insatiable desire of a curious child, hungry for more, and *more*, and **more**!!! Are bugs to God like toys are to children—you can never have enough? Is God a compulsive, bells-and-whistles-out-of-control creator, never knowing when "enough is *enough*, already!"?

I am awed and tickled by the parallel universe populated by a myriad of tiny creatures flitting and fluttering around me, and—intelligent though I be—I am obtusely oblivious to its intricate, bustling existence. I have been reading about bees[24] —another universe I have been blind to, except for when a bee buzzes too close for my comfort—which undoubtedly has sensitized my mind to the winged world at this moment in time. What parallels might I see between my life and the life of the night creatures buzzing my reading light?

Spiritually, I am drawn to the Light and the warmth of God's love. Intellectually, I revel in bathing myself in new ideas and perspectives, basking in energizing enlightenment. Emotionally, I occasionally find myself enveloped by the darkness of depression or loneliness and seek out people and experiences that lighten my heart. Relationally, I like to gather with others of my species to cheer on the Little Leaguers or absorb divine Light amid the buzz of fellowship. Light is essential to my existence on many levels, and like my light-crazed companions on this sultry eve, I am bewitched and bedazzled by Light wherever I may find It.

> "Why on earth does God need so many different kinds of bugs? It must be that God has the insatiable desire of a curious child..."

I wonder, in these moments when I am drawn to the spotlight of Grace, am I, also, a tiny creature crashing unceremoniously into another being's universe, inviting them to shift focus and experience God's grace in a new way? Do they marvel over my intricacy and chuckle over my pesky presence? Am I the light of another being's world, as Christ has called me to be? Am I most like a beetle, well protected by a shiny, iridescent, impermeable shell, or am I like the teeny-tiny, delicate bug whose wings and body are vulnerable and transparent? Am I satisfied to rest in the Light or do I flutter about, seeking who knows what? Where do I go when the source of my light is snuffed out?

Gracious God, may I always have the good sense to rest in your Light and may I be a reflection of your Light, to those around me.

---

24 The Secret Lives of Bees, a delightful novel by Sue Monk Kidd, led me to The Queen Must Die and Other Affairs of Bees and Men (be honest now, who could resist such a title!), by beekeeper, William Longgood.

 # *Poison Ivy*

While walking with the woman in the garden, the Master Gardener said, "You are free to enjoy all that you see, but you must not touch the three-leafed vine that crawls along the garden path and meanders up the trees, for when you touch it, it will surely make you itch."

You would think I'd learn! But here I sit, I-T-C-H-I-N-G!!! I'm a little like Eve. I can't resist going into places where the beautiful yet poisonous ivy lays in wait for me. "Come into the woods," she whispers softly and bewitchingly, like the Sirens in the Odyssey, and off I traipse, thinking to myself, "I'll be careful. I know what Poison Ivy looks like. I'll just avoid it."

In the good old days, I was not allergic to Poison Ivy. Unlike my husband—who has been highly allergic to it since childhood—I used to be able to pull entire plants out of the garden with my bare hands without any ramifications. Then one summer, that all changed. I almost went crazy from the itching, my body splotched everywhere with nasty blotches of the plague. From then on, Poison Ivy was the enemy and I trembled with fear every time I spied any plant with three leaves.

I have since learned to recognize it from other plants of similar design and now venture into the woods or garden with a healthy respect for my enemy, my eyes alert, keeping my hands to myself. A nature-loving pastor once suggested that I wash with Fels Naptha soap after being in the woods, and I follow this pastoral advice religiously.

Yesterday, however, I experienced a lapse in caution and judgment. I love to pull weeds. Crazy, I know, but it's just one of my silly quirks. I went out into the garden behind our house—a small shady area that butts up against the edge of the cliff on which our house perches—on a mission. When we first moved here, the flower bed was separated from the woods by a wide border of myrtle that had been planted on the slope. In two year's time, the wild flowers and weeds have encroached upon the tamed area of myrtle. I decided to "rescue" the myrtle by thinning out some of the less attractive plants, thus providing the myrtle with additional exposure to the sun and more space in which to spread.

Obviously, at some point, I came into contact with the enemy and, in spite of the fact that I went into the house several times to wash with Fels Naptha, I am now itching and scratching. You'd think I'd learn! Even though it may seem that playing in my garden and catching Poison Ivy is minor in comparison to Eve plucking fruit from the tree of knowledge of good and evil, we both knew we were "playing with fire." Eve knew better. So did I. My wisdom and self-control genes reflect that the apple doesn't fall far from the tree!

I have a similar weakness when it comes to devouring chocolate. If I had been the woman created from Adam's rib, I would have gotten us into the same heap of trouble if the fruit of the tree had been chocolate—*God*iva, of course! In truth, I have scads of weaknesses that lead me into poisonous patches in the ivy of life. Our actions have consequences, some more costly than others, but fortunately, there is Grace:

> *For I am convinced that neither death nor life, neither angels*
> *nor demons, neither the present nor the future, nor any powers,*
> *neither height nor depth, nor anything else in all creation*
> *(not even Poison Ivy!), will be able to separate us from the love*
> *of God that is in Christ Jesus our Lord. Romans 8:38-39 NIV*

God loved Adam and Eve so much, that he revised his original plan to counteract the consequences of their disobedience. Jesus suffered the death and separation from God that Adam and Eve had been warned of, while Adam and Eve were allowed to live, albeit in a world now riddled with pain and evil. God, in his mercy and grace, continued to walk with them—and all of their ancestors.

I feel closest to God when I am in the woods. Alas, my "Garden of Eden" was a figment of my imagination, leading me to believe that I—on my own wits—could outsmart Ivy. As God and I walk together, I mindlessly—and sometimes even mindfully—venture off the path, stumbling over fallen branches, tripping on tree roots and falling into contact with thorn bushes and nettles, bumping my head on low hanging limbs, and, yes, traipsing into patches of Poison Ivy lurking among the wildflowers. How the Creator must smirk and giggle at my clumsiness and foolishness! And yet, God still continues to be my walking buddy through the pain of Poison Ivy and the pain of loss or disappointment, through the wild thorn bushes and a multitude of thorny, scratchy situations in my daily life.

Watch where you're stepping!!!

Chapter IV

Floppy, Flawed, and In Need of Grace

My grace is sufficient for you,
for my power is made perfect in weakness.
2 Corinthians 12:9 NIV

In life as in the dance, grace glides on blistered feet.
~ Alice Abrams[25]

God uses cracked pots.
~ Patsy Clairmont[26]

Grace was in all her steps,
Heaven in her eye.
In Every gesture dignity and love.
~ John Milton[27]

When our knowledge coalesces with
our humanity and our humor, it can add up to wisdom.
~ Carol Orlock[28]

25 Abrams, Alice, American goldsmith and jewelry designer. Used with permission of the author.
26 Clairmont, Patsy, God Uses Cracked Pots, Focus on the Family, 1991.
27 John Milton, 1608-1674, English poet and author of "Paradise Lost".
28 Warner, Carolyn, Ed., Treasury of Women's Quotations, Prentice Hall, 1992, p. 171.

The Gift of Feeling Floppier

We have different gifts, according to the grace given us.
Romans 12:6 NIV

I am an exceptionally gifted person. Lest you think I am bragging, look closely at the title of this essay. I have been blessed with many "teachable moments" in the "gifted and talented" class of life. There was a period of time— a very *l-o-n-g* time period—in which I perceived myself as a failure. In spite of the fact that I was obviously a smart, and moderately talented, child and teen, my faulty radar zeroed in primarily on what I perceived as my numerous faults and failings. While my self-esteem has vastly improved with age, like a fine cheese or wine, I still revisit that place of shame and insecurity now and again.

> "What a relief it is to 'break through all that held breath and isometric tension about needing to look good."

Once I finally comprehended that failure is a natural part of life, and that failure really is the best teacher, I was able to relax into the experience and actually learn from my mistakes. What a relief it is to "break through all that held breath and isometric tension about needing to look good,"[29] declares Anne Lamott. It requires buckets of energy to hold in my emotional gut and pretend I'm perfect—or at least appear to be "fine" about *not* being perfect. It is humanly impossible to both look good, and learn, all in the same breath. It's like trying to rub your head and pat your tummy simultaneously.

Middle age has helped me make peace with my fallibility. When my dad hit middle age, his fashion sense and dignity flew out the window. He began wearing loud plaid slacks—which clashed with his striped shirts (burgundy stripes with orange and teal plaid, no less!)—and goofy looking golf hats, causing his adolescent daughter no end of embarrassment. The man had a closet full of dignified suits, stylish sports coats and beautiful ties, and always looked sharp for work and church. It was only on weekends that he appeared to be totally color blind, throwing caution to the fashion wind.

---

29 Lamott, Anne, <u>Traveling Mercies: Some Thoughts on Faith</u>, Anchor Books/Random House, Inc., 1999.

With middle age, I achieved a level of comfort with myself that allowed me to relax and not need to always look my best. While I would *never* pair stripes and plaids, I am able to appear in public occasionally with my hair askew, no make-up, and sloppy, mismatched clothes. I now realize that my dad's choice of attire had more to do with his self-acceptance than it ever did with style and fashion. What still puzzles me, though, is that Dad actually seemed to think plaids and stripes looked great together! Maybe there is another middle-age plateau waiting for me up the hill and around the corner.

Anne Lamott would call this "the gift of feeling floppier." I have a beautiful crocheted angel that my mother-in-law made for me whose wings grow droopy over time from the Indiana humidity. Evidently, looking after my household is quite a strain for her! Periodically, Mom takes "Gracie" home to dip her in starch to restore her angelic stature. It really doesn't bother me when Gracie's wings give out. Her floppiness is endearing. Like Gracie, I fly on floppy wings. Always have. Always will. So I might as well dress the part!

Embracing floppiness isn't an endorsement of laziness or underachievement. It's an affirmation of the dance between divinity and humanity; the dance between lithe Grace and pigeon-toed Linda. I "glide on blistered feet." Like a daddy dancing with his little girl, Grace allows me to put my feet atop of hers as she spins and twirls, occasionally lifting me up and swinging me round and round, smiling as I squeal with delight.

I've learned that my dancing ability is far less important in comparison to the grace with which I take my falls. I'm a Red Skelton dancer, tripping over my oversized, two left feet, dressed like a clown, a stupid grin on my face. Like one of those life-sized dancing dolls of my childhood—a spineless rag doll that attaches to a child's feet with elastic—I come to life and dance, only by God's grace. And still, Grace invites me to dance! Go figure!

The Last Shall Be First

So the last will be first, and the first will be last.
Matthew 20:16 NIV

The Bible is rife with paradox. Take the parable of the workers in the vineyard, for example, in Matthew 20:12-16. This is the story of the landowner who hired men to work for a day's wage of a denarius. At the third, sixth, ninth, and eleventh hours he hired additional workers. Why? Because they were standing around idle with nothing to do! Then, at the end of the day, he paid every single worker a denarius. Imagine the uproar this caused!

In today's world, people would be crying discrimination and contacting their attorneys and labor unions. While it's common for us to sagely quip to each other less-than-sympathetically, "Life is not fair!" from little on, we tend to be obsessed with fairness. "It's not fair!" cries the six-year-old when his toddler sister is allowed to play with *his* toys. "Why does *Johnny* get to stay out late?" bemoans the seventeen-year-old. "You *never* let *me* stay out that late when *I was* thirteen! That is *so* not fair!" When someone cuts in line in front of us, or we get a speeding ticket when "everyone else" is speeding too, we grumble to ourselves about the unfairness. Our judicial system has a library full of tomes replete with laws meant to guarantee fairness "under the law."

From the child who spies another child's red sucker and decides his green one isn't as good, to the adult peering jealously over the privacy fence at the neighbors shiny new boat, we are obsessed with fairness, are we not? No wonder the concept of grace is so hard for us to grasp. Grace just plain isn't fair! But then, if grace was fair—it wouldn't be grace, now would it?

In a nutshell, this unsettling parable is about how we can show up late in the day and receive God's grace in full measure. What a deal! That is, unless we've been one of "the faithful" who showed up at the crack of dawn and toiled all day. Then we're sure to grumble! We like to see ourselves as faithful servants, but all too often we show up late, tired and distracted, and labor half-heartedly. Or even worse, we oversleep or hang out in front of the TV and don't even bother to check in with the Boss to get our working orders for the day. God's response? Grace. Our cups, filled to the brim; overflowing.

What a deal!

"But then, if grace was fair
- it wouldn't be grace,
now would it?"

Tangles

Wherever there is life, there is twist and mess.
~ Annie Dillard[30]

I am *not* fond of tangles. Nor am I patient with them. They really slow me down, put a frown on my face, and send me into a bad mood! Years ago when I was an avid knitter, I dealt with many a tangle. My Aunt Marge taught me to wind every skein of yarn into a ball before I used it. Everything would go fine until the end of the skein when inevitably I would create a tangled mess out of the last few yards. A born perfectionist, raised under the Puritan dictum to, "waste not, want not," I would labor over those tangles until, finally, every inch of yarn on the skein was successfully transferred to the large, orderly ball.

When my daughter, Beth, was born, I couldn't wait until her hair was long enough to put into pigtails and braids. I, of course, did not think about what her baby-fine, silky tresses would be like to contend with in the morning, following ten or more hours of tossing and turning. After her bath, as I would comb out tangle after tangle, the fresh, fruity fragrance of the "Tangle Free" spritz would often transport me back to myself at her age, wrapped in a bath towel, standing patiently while my father (Yes, my father!) would comb out my tangles.

I remember these times with Daddy fondly and assumed that he enjoyed them also. Now I wonder if he, too, grumbled under his breath at me to "*Please*, stand still!" and I realize what a labor of love and patience this liberated father of the fifties performed.

I've also found myself in emotional tangles, my feelings all jumbled and hard to sort out. I think I spent the bulk of my teenage years in such a tangled jungle! And then there's the tangle of relationships: teenage triangles—love triangles and triangles between girls in which one is always feeling left out (some people never outgrow such entanglements!); mother-daughter conflicts; father-son stand-offs; gender and generation gaps; work, social, religious, friend, and foe relationships… Human entanglements make a ball of yarn and curly locks seem like veritable blessings!

In spite of my distaste for tangles, I find them a useful metaphor when talking with clients about the messiness of life. The thought that life is like a skein of yarn, which can eventually, with time and effort, but not without frustrations and fears, be untangled, offers hope in the midst of tangles. To know that one can "untangle" when feeling ready to "unravel" offers a sturdy lifeline in times of chaos and confusion.

Anyone who has ever worked with yarn knows just how strong a strand of yarn is. If you separate the plies, you may be able to pull apart a single ply. But woven together, the triple-strand is amazingly strong. People are that way, too. We have internal strands in which our strengths are woven together into who we are. And we have external strands consisting of other people who weave around us and provide strength when our lives are frayed and stretched to the limit.

---

30 Dillard, Annie, <u>Pilgrim at Tinker's Creek</u>,, Harper & Row Publishers, 1974, p. 138.

*T*here *is* one kind of tangle that I *do* like and that is the tangle of nature. While God created a bounty of botanical beauty, you'll not find anything in the wild, untouched-by-human-hands environs that even closely resembles a neatly manicured garden.

> *Wherever there is life, there is twist and mess: the frizz of an arctic lichen the tangle of brush along a bank, the dogleg of a dog's leg, the way a line has got to curve, split, or knob. The planet is characterized by its very jaggedness, its random heaps of mountains, its frayed fringes of shore...*[31]

If we can get past our frustrations, we will discover an unfathomable beauty that has been rendered invisible by our impatience and our sense of entitlement for life to proceed in an orderly, smooth, and predictable fashion—according to *our* expectations.

> *The texture of the world, its filigree and scrollwork, means that there is the possibility for beauty here, a beauty inexhaustible in its complexity, which opens to my knock, which answers in me a call I do not remember calling, and which trains me to the wild and extravagant nature of the spirit I seek.*[32]

I've always pictured the Garden of Eden as something you'd see on "The Homes of the Rich and Famous," and Adam and Eve as models of perfection—not quite Ken and Barbie, but close. Is it possible that God never intended his creation to be "perfect," but to be beautiful in its very messiness? The idea that life is not meant to be perfect—that real life is adorned with tangled frizz, awakens with sleep in its eyes and bad breath, and steps out in sweats and torn tennies *really* appeals to me.

How about you?

---

31 Dillard, Annie, Pilgrim at Tinker's Creek, Harper & Row Publishers, 1974, p. 138.
32 Dillard, Annie, Pilgrim at Tinker's Creek, Harper & Row Publishers, 1974, p. 139.

Winter Rainbows

And God said, "...I have set my rainbow in the clouds,
and it will be the sign of the covenant between me and the earth.
...Never again will the waters become a flood to destroy all life.
Whenever the rainbow appears in the clouds I will see it
and remember the everlasting covenant between God
and all living creatures of every kind on the earth."
Genesis 9:12-16 NIV

Deep in thought for the day ahead, I set out early for work unaware of my surroundings. I have not yet shaken off my morning fog, but as I drive, I begin to go over my plans. Suddenly, my inner child tugs at the skirt of my awareness, drawing my attention to the Grandma Moses wintry scene in which I am myself a character.

Around me, a gentle fog provides a milky-blue backdrop against which everything—every leafless bush, every barren tree, each brown blade of grass in the field—is dusted white. My eyes open with wonder and leaning forward into this landscape, I say aloud, "Lord, this is beautiful! It is *so* beautiful!" How long can this beauty last, I wonder. I feel an urgency to drink in this softness and peace; to somehow hold onto this rare encounter with a winter grace, for it has worked a miracle in my heart.

I arrive at work too quickly. I long to stay outside, suspended in time in this wonderland. As I regretfully open my van door, I am met with yet another captivating sight. A shower of ice crystals cascades like a waterfall from a nearby tree, each crystal dancing excitedly in the crisp air. And as the rays of morning sun intersect with the delicate crystals, they become prisms, refracting into thousands of miniature rainbows of sparkling, shooting color. I am captivated by the kaleidoscope of rainbows, dizzied by the scene as each tiny miracle vies for my attention, and I stare in childlike wonder. I imagine chubby, rosy-cheeked cherubs tossing bundles of rainbows into the heavens like confetti, with wild abandon, unable to contain their joy. Each rainbow carries God's promise of his healing, transforming presence.

My heart has been heavy of late. I have been struggling to be at peace with myself and with my Father. In a few short minutes on an ordinary morning, My Father spoke to me in extraordinary ways. His message was of joy, excitement, hope, promise, new beginnings, energy: LIFE!

70 X 7

Lord, how many times shall I forgive my brother
when he sins against me? Up to Seven times?
Matthew 18:21 NIV

I'm no math wiz, but I know the answer to this arithmetical puzzle posed to Jesus by his disciple, Peter: "70 X 7!"[33] Easy to compute. Difficult to do. Was Jesus saying we must literally forgive someone 490 times? I think the point He was trying to make was about the *spirit* of forgiveness; about cultivating a forgiving heart. What are some of your earliest memories involving forgiveness? Here's a peek at one of mine:

"Mom! Mikey hit me!"

"I did not! I barely tapped her. She won't leave my stuff alone!"

"That's not true! I was just sitting here watching the Mickey Mouse Club and he leaned over on my side of the couch and slugged me! Make him go to his room!!!"

"Michael, tell your little sister you're sorry."

"Heck, no! She's such a brat!"

"Michael, uncross you're arms and wipe that glare off your face and tell your sister you're sorry!"

"I'm sorry—you little rat!"

"MICHAEL FRANCIS!"

"Okay, okay! 'I'm s-o-r-r-y.'"

"That's better, thank you. " Now, Linda, tell Mikey you forgive him."

"WHY?"

"Because I said so!"

"I don't want to!"

"Jesus says we're to forgive—now forgive your brother right NOW!"

"I forgive you—you dirty rotten tomato!"

"LINDA CAROL!"

"Okay, okay! *I forgive you.*"

"What? I couldn't hear you."

"I forgive you."

"Thank you. Now could the two of you please get along so I can get supper on the table by the time your father gets home?"

Let me guess, you can practically substitute your own family names and the dialog fits to a tee! Apologizing and forgiving are bugaboos from the get-go for most, if not all, of us. And it doesn't necessarily get any easier with age, does it? How do we cultivate a forgiving heart?

A heart that produces the fruit of forgiveness is one that knows the fragrant rain of having been forgiven. It is a heart that struggles continually with the weeds and thorns of pride and self-righteousness. Forgiveness blossoms *with time*, growing slowly *over time*, unfolding, delicate petal, by delicate petal. It cannot be forced to bloom, like a hot house flower. But when its time has come, it is a gift of grace— and it is well worth the effort—for all involved.

"Ouch!!! M-O-M-M-Y! Mikey hit me again!"

---

33 Jesus said to him, "I do not say to you, up to seven times, but up to seventy times seven." Matthew 18:22 NASB

Chapter V

All In the Family

Friendship Tea[34]
(for Bethany)

Sipping Friendship Tea with me
Reading Riley's poetry
Lost together in the rhyme
Losing track of evening's time.

Stumbling over words so quaint
Enjoying pictures that they paint
Sharing tales of friendship true
Discovering friends in me and you.

A poetess and protégé
Create an image on this day
That finds its way into my poem
That springs from mother-heart's rich loam.

If you can't get rid of the family skeleton,
you may as well make it dance.
~ *George Bernard Shaw*[35]

---

34 Bethany and I spent many precious moments together when she was young reading poetry. She
   especially liked James Whitcomb Riley and Emily Dickinson. I think it was the cadence that captured
   and enthralled her. She still enjoys my homemade Friendship Tea.
35 Used with permission of the Estate of George Bernard Shaw.

Strawberry Fields Forever

Then God said, "Let the land produce vegetation: seed-bearing plants and trees on the land that bear fruit with seed in it, according to their various kinds." And it was so... And God saw that it was good.

Genesis 1:11-12 NIV

*O*ne hot, summer day, when I was a little girl, my daddy introduced me to the delicious hunt for strawberries. We were visiting Grandma and Grandpa Reuman, my mother's parents, in Attica, New York. Their large home—hand built by Grandpa—overlooked a picturesque valley. I doubt that Dad and I talked much out there in the field behind the house, but just being with him and having him all to myself was a real treat. I couldn't resist popping a few of the reddest and juiciest sun-warmed treasures into my mouth right there in the field.

Suddenly, the muted, country quiet was broken by an alarm sounding from Attica State Prison, far off in the valley, alerting the community that a prisoner had escaped. The harsh sound scared me to death, and I just knew that the escapee would come get me! Dad tried to allay my fears, explaining that the occasional escapee was usually a "trustee," a prisoner who was trusted enough to work outside the wall. Such prisoners were typically due to get out of prison soon, but the security of what was familiar was more appealing than freedom, so they'd head downtown to a bar and wait to be captured, successfully extending their tenure. My fears were soothed and we enjoyed our berries with Grandma's homemade shortcake.

Strawberries have always been a vital part of my summers, even when I did not have easy access to a strawberry field. During the summer, our neighborhood was frequented several times a week by a truck laden with berries. I got just as excited when I heard this truck coming as I did for the ice cream truck (well, almost). These luscious, locally grown berries sold for the tempting price of four quarts for a dollar. Mom would make shortcake and we'd top it all off with a generous spritz of Reddi-Wip. Dad registered his appreciation with groans of delight and lots of lip-smacking.

Before moving to Anderson, my husband and I lived in Northern Michigan where I went berry picking around the 4th of July. When we returned to Indiana, I couldn't wait for July to come around, only to discover that I was a month late. You can bet I didn't make that mistake twice!

When my parents retired and moved to Anderson to be near my family, Dad and I took up pickin' once again. For several years, we went to a local fruit and vegetable farm, oftentimes accompanied by my kids, Matt and Beth, who were as young as I was when I picked my first berry. Later, Dad put in a big garden next to his condo, a generous portion of it dedicated to strawberries.

Bethie and Grandpa loved to trek out to the strawberry patch where Beth would load up her t-shirt with berries and bring them in, thrilled with her payload. It was a special time between little Beth and Grandpa, reminiscent of my own special times with my strawberry-loving papa. I plan to take my own grandkids pickin' someday!

Exodus 20:5-6 (NIV) tells us that God promises his love "to a thousand generations of those who love me and keep my commandments." Just think: when we receive God's love and respond with obedience, we pass God's love on to the next one thousand generations! Is "a thousand generations" simply a metaphor to emphasize the abundance and availability of God's love? I don't know. But if the flapping of a butterfly's wings in Indiana can impact the ecosystem in China, then I certainly think God's love has its own eternal "butterfly effect."

Just as we receive a legacy from our Heavenly Father, our own family legacies are also passed on. Enjoying strawberries together is a love-filled legacy, a crimson thread in the enduring weaving that is my family. Such a simple act of grace! Every Father's Day—appropriately celebrated during strawberry season—I fondly remember my strawberry-loving father, Frank Elmore. Thanks for the legacy, Dad!

Glue

Man is born broken. He lives by mending.
The grace of God is the glue.
Eugene O'Neill[36]

*I*n junior high, one of my art projects involved creating a mosaic picture. We cut strips of colored construction paper and then snipped the strips into hundreds of colorful squares. The challenge was to *neatly* arrange the squares, keeping the glue contained to the under surface only. I became terribly frustrated when the glue would seep out under the edges of the squares. No matter how carefully I daubed at the errant glue, inevitably it would slyly slink up on top of the carefully placed squares. My attempts at removing the excess glue often resulted in the edges of the squares fraying, the colors fading. Overall, the mosaic looked good, but under close inspection, my battle with the glue was readily apparent.

Glue is a fascinating item to children. They love to taste it, feel its gooey, sticky texture, and use it generously to hold together their artistic expressions. As a child I *loved* the delicious fragrance of school paste and the mysterious chemical odor of rubber cement. Then came the wonders of mess-free glue stick, amazing super glue, and, my personal favorite, stick-it notes. (These little notes are the glue that keeps my life running smoothly!) Many everyday tasks are simplified and eased thanks to the wonders of glue.

My family is a work of art in progress, an intricate tapestry of entangled, sturdy yet fraying relational strands. As in all families, the processes of breakdown and mending are ongoing and inseparable. Our conversations and behaviors are often a little rough around the edges, our nerves frayed from the stress of life. No matter how many mental stick-it notes I post reminding me to listen attentively, think before I act, remain calm, I still sometimes speak carelessly, inadvertently (and, yes, sometimes intentionally), straining or tearing the delicate relational fibers.

Just as frustrating is when the glue holding my loved ones together gives way and I watch helplessly from the sidelines. My therapeutic pocket is stuffed with an array of relational adhesives, but my help may not be welcomed or appropriate. It hurts to see the glue dissolve, causing relationships around me to become unstable, if even only temporarily. I want to nose my way in and daub on some of my own glue.

36 O'Neill, Eugene, "The Great God Brown," Act IV, scene I, in <u>Collected Works</u>, Random House, Ed.

Life is much like the messy, frustrating process of creating a mosaic. Somehow, though, Grace takes our messy moments and composes beauty. Even though our relationships are strained by our sinful, wounded natures, they prove amazingly resilient when infused with the presence of Grace.

When I'm wise enough to not run for my Elmer's, I simply listen and be present, prayerfully trusting that a greater Glue is at work in unseen ways. I strive and struggle to trust that the troubling tears and frayed edges are important pieces of the relational mosaic, a masterpiece in progress, being held together with the right Glue. It's no small miracle when I arrive at this peaceful, Grace-filled haven. Anne Lamott shares these wise words of her pastor: "The world sometimes feels like the emergency ward and that we who are more or less OK for now need to take the tenderest possible care of the more wounded people in the waiting room, until the healer comes. *You sit with people and bring them juice and graham crackers.*"[37]

It's not that we should never jump in and "do something." The key is to know when to jump and when to sit. More often that not, sitting is by far the best choice—and the hardest. We are all products of a "quick fix" society and sitting and waiting is painful. We like to think we have the answers, that we are in control of life, but the truth is, we don't, and we aren't.

Anne Lamott, in speaking about her church family and the process of "sitting with" says, "we offered the gift of no comfort when there being no comfort was where they had landed."[38] To sit with *you* means that *I* have to realize that I, too, am in that emergency ward, and sooner or later, *I* will be the patient. Like it or not, we will all land where there is no comfort. That's scary. And we'll need someone to sit with us in that seemingly God-forsaken place so the Glue can be applied and set up.

I don't know about you, but I am *very* glad for the spiritual adhesive of Grace, in my family, in my church family, and in the emergency ward of life.

"Would you care for some juice and crackers?"

Pleasant words are a honeycomb,
sweet to the soul and healing to the bones.
Proverbs 16:24 NIV

37 Lamott, Anne, Traveling Mercies: Some Thoughts on Faith, Anchor Books, 1999, p. 106.
38 Lamott, Anne, Traveling Mercies: Some Thoughts on Faith, Anchor Books, 1999, p. 152.

Snot and Grace

Love bears all things...
I Corinthians 13:7 NKJV

I know, I know! I've gone too far this time, stepped over the line of decency, causing Emily Post to turn over in her grave. Could I have chosen a more disgusting topic? To put things in perspective, unless you'd like to hear some of my brother Michael's stories about autopsies and cadavers (during his tenure in medical school I had to endure such information over dinner!), then I suggest that you give me a few paragraphs to see what I can do with my less than savory topic. I have a couple of vignettes that demonstrate how tolerance for snot is a sure sign of grace:

Awhile back, I was visiting with my good friend, Sandra, and her two young children in the living room of their home when Caleb, her youngest, unobtrusively sidled up to his mother, as we were chatting, and rubbed his snotty nose on her sleeve. Now, you could say that he didn't know any better, which perhaps he didn't, but the crucial point, I think, is that a mother's love "bears all things," including snotty sleeves, saliva-soaked shoulders, a lap full of runny poop (on her Sunday suit, of course), a face squirted with warm pee, and the volcanic eruptions of a child's partially digested stomach (of candy, pop, corn on the cob, and cotton candy following a hot, hectic day at the carnival). And she gracefully bears such indignities with dignity and grace. A Congressional Medal of Honor is *definitely* in order.

My second example transpired one warm, sunny, summer afternoon while boating. Rex had just boarded the boat dripping wet, having slalomed around the lake, and was toweling off when our newly acquired daughter-in-law, Kristy, informed him that he had snot on his face. Now, snot on one's face following skiing—especially if you've done a nose dive and taken in a face full of lake water—is not uncommon. But passing on such delicate information to one's new father-in-law is significant, to say the least. Obviously, Kristy felt comfortable enough with "Dad" to broach the subject and take it upon herself to inform him that he needed to wipe his nose. And "Dad's" gracious acceptance of her remark was equally as significant. I remember commenting, as we all laughed, that this was a sign that Kristy was truly one of the family.

And so, I believe I've quite adequately demonstrated the subtle, graceful connection between snot and grace. Metaphorically speaking, life is full of moments when our noses run, catching us unawares and unprepared without a tissue or handkerchief handy. How we handle those moments, both as the one caught in the act of being human, and as an observer of the flaws and frailties of others, reflects our ability to give and receive grace.

I can't think of any passages in the Bible that talk about snot (thank goodness!), but Scripture certainly has a great deal to say about God's abiding love and grace. The realization that we are loved and of great value comes, on rare occasions, in the form of an eye-opening, lightning bolt experience – a dramatic exclamation point lighting up the sky of our hearts. Much more frequently, though, a slowly dawning awareness that we are deeply loved is nurtured in the day-in, day-out showers of tiny droplets of human love reflecting God's incredible love for us. To be able to rub one's nose on Mama's or Papa's sleeve, or to feel secure enough in one's new family to be forthright (with tact, respect, and a dash of humor, of course), speaks of love on the grassroots level. This is love that grows imperceptibly, day by day, rooting itself firmly in rich, well-prepared, sun-warmed, heart-soil: *embodied grace.*

Isn't it good to know that even when we're feeling or acting snotty, we can sidle up to our Heavenly Father and... well, you get the picture!

Incarcerated

I am the gate; whoever enters through me will be saved.
He will come in and go out, and find pasture.
John 10:9 NIV

*O*ne summer afternoon, while soaking and floating in Adams Lake with my school day buddies, Lea and Kathy, we engaged in storytelling about—what else—our kids. "My favorite story of Matt," Lea announces, chuckling, "is of how Rex and Linda had to gate him into his room at night with THREE gates!" I'm sure Kathy has heard this story before, but it is also one of my favorites, so I readily share the details.

Matt learned to walk early (way too early, in my opinion!) and strongly objected to any form of containment. Climbing in and out of (or on top of) just about anything was his forte' at a very early age. At around age two, he decided that the crib was more a vehicle than a stationery object best utilized for slumber. By shaking the crib, he discovered that he could masterfully maneuver it across the shag carpet to within arms reach of the dresser. His goal: the jar of Vaseline, which works quite nicely for creative expression on all sorts of surfaces.

> "Does God get exasperated with us, impatient with our immature behavior?"

Not to be outwitted, Rex and I craftily removed the wheels and chuckled with delight as we lay him down for his nap. Not a problem! Matt quickly learned that he could escape the crib by climbing over the bars with the wall at his back to keep him from falling. However, without the wheels, he would become stuck between the wall and the crib and we were afraid he might hang himself. So, it was back to the drawing board.

Feeling somewhat defeated, yet ever hopeful, we removed the crib from his room, placed the mattress on the floor and tried every psychological trick we could think of to convince Matt that he was now a big boy and ready to sleep in (and *stay put* in) a big boy bed. Matt reveled in his new-found freedom, wandering the house from the minute we put him down. Not to be outwitted (yet, again!), we placed a baby gate in his doorway. No problema! He loved to climb and joyfully took the challenge like a squirrel to a squirrel-proof bird-feeder.

The gauntlet was thrown! A second gate was installed above the first gate. But freedom still remained a mere scramble away. Rex wanted to just close and lock the door, but I couldn't bear the thought of locking my child up or of not being able to peek in and check up on him. So a third gate was purchased and the doorway was now impenetrable. We definitely won this round, but at quite an emotional cost.

Have you any idea how guilty a parent can feel upon discovery of one's two-year-old curled up on the floor, by the gated doorway, tightly hugging his blankie and stuffed monkey, sound asleep, looking so sweet and innocent? Trust me, it's traumatic. But hey, incarceration worked! We could work through the trauma.

The new nightly routine now became a process of setting up camp for Matt at his doorway, settling him down for a story and prayers, the designated parent of the evening sitting cross-legged in the hallway. After kisses, gates one, two, and three were installed. Some nights, the inmate would scream and holler and other nights, he accepted his incarceration peacefully. Eventually, the gates were no longer needed (I can't remember if this was when he was around four – or sixteen…)

Twenty-six years later, the parental guilt has abated, and Matt does not seem to have been too terribly traumatized. Matt is married now and we look forward to someday having grandchildren—we just hope he has a child "just like" him!

I wonder, do our Heavenly Father, Jesus, and the Holy Spirit ever hang out, like Lea, Kathy, and I—floating on a cloud, perhaps—swapping stories about their children?

"Hey, did you hear that Linda locked her keys in the car *again*—that makes *three* times this summer! And this time the dog was in the car! What on earth would she do without our rescue service?"

"Oh, I can top that! Did you hear the one about when Rex…?"

"If you think that's funny, just listen to this!"

I imagine that, from God's perspective, we often act like two year olds, in need of constant parental vigil and ingenuity. Does God get exasperated with us, impatient with our immature behavior? (Just check out some of the Old Testament stories about the Israelites and you'll know that he does!) Does God heave a big sigh of relief when we're safely tucked into bed at night, knowing we've made it through another day of shenanigans?

Daily, I am tempted to climb over the gates erected by my heavenly parent to keep me safely contained. Sometimes I actually make an escape. But like the time when I was five or six and climbed over the backyard gate—and caught and tore my pants on a picket—my escapes are less than graceful. While I crave freedom, and desire to be my own boss, ultimately I know that living in God's gated community is in my best interest.

Chapter VI

Grace Across Borders

MISSION

The spirit of Christ is the spirit of missions. The nearer we get to Him,
the more intensely missionary we become.
~ Henry Martyn[39]

The primary mission of VOSH is to facilitate the provision of eye care
worldwide to people who can neither afford nor obtain such care.
Mission Statement
Volunteer Optometric Services to Humanity[40]

EXILE

You shall leave behind all that you love most dearly,
and this is the arrow that the bow of exile shoots first.
You shall find out how bitter someone else's bread tastes,
and how hard is the way up and down another's stairs.
Dante, Paradise (Canto XVII, 55-60)[41]

Exile is more than a crossing of borders…it is a journey to one's self.
James Madison University Scholars[42]

---

39 Henry Martyn, 1781-1812, was a Bible translator and missionary to India and Persia.
40 http://www.vosh-indiana.org/mission.htm.
41 Dante Alighieri (1265-1321), Italian poet.
42 Madison, the magazine for James Madison University, Ed., Pam Brock, Winter 2003, "Living in Exile."

Ambassadors for Christ

Go to the village ahead of you, and at once you will find a donkey tied there, with her colt with her. Untie them and bring them to me. If anyone says anything to you, tell them the Lord needs them.
Matthew 21:2-3 NIV

A winding, gravel road weaves it's way up a mountainside in Honduras, sparsely traveled, except for an occasional four wheel vehicle, people on foot, and herds of cattle. We are in Honduras as part of a medical mission team with Volunteer Optometric Services to Humanity (VOSH). My eye doctor husband, Rex, and I, and one other optometrist, have opted to spend our "free day" taking a side trip into the mountains to do a mini-clinic.

Our adventure began several hours earlier with we three gringos waiting eagerly (and, yes, impatiently—Latino time and U.S. time are *not* in sync with each other) for our ride, perspiring in the already warm morning sun, as we paced the busy sidewalk outside the Grand Sula Hotel in downtown San Pedro Sula. We had been told that our driver would speak no English, so we were

> "I had never thought of myself as an ass before..."

wondering how on earth we'd recognize him, and vice versa. Never disappointed by the creativity demonstrated by the Hondurans, it was my keen vision that noticed our last name—Teeple—written in the dust on the back windshield of his vehicle.

Once loaded into the time-worn, oversized van, we set out, leaving the noisy city behind as we ventured out into the countryside and up into the mountains. Rex was pleasantly surprised to discover that he was able to carry on a chummy conversation with our chauffeur. We stopped once in a small town, where our amiable driver knocked on a door and asked if his passenger, the señora, could please use the "el baño." I'm not certain whether he actually knew the resident, but the Hondurans are a very gracious people, so my need was taken care of.

We stopped one more time, higher up the mountain, to transfer to an open bed truck to traverse the more rugged road ahead. I was given the seat of honor in the cab with el señor driver while the men bounced around in the back. My view wasn't quite as good as theirs, but I was a whole lot more comfy!

Weaving up the mountain, small dwellings, made of whatever can be found to create walls and a roof, nestle along the roadside. Pineapple fields dot the mountainside and beautiful vistas of the Honduran peaks and valleys surprise and delight us. Our journey was delayed briefly due to a cow and her calf taking their share out of the middle of the road, but Rex came to our rescue and convinced the travelers to share the road.

Arriving at our destination of Canchias, we discover a quaint little village with humble dwellings. To our surprise, we also find a wonderful mission—a compound lovingly built there by *Heart to Honduras*. This Christian compound includes a school, a church, a modest store, a care center where the handicapped children of the village are cared for, a medical clinic, and a ministry center where Honduran pastors gather several times a year for training and renewal.

The logo of this mission is the ass. Miquel Pinell, the director of Heart to Honduras, explained to us that over the years the word "ass" has been vulgarized. The mission's symbol proclaims their willingness to be used by Christ in service to others. Smiling, Miquel pointed out that the word ass is right in the middle of the word amb*ass*ador. What a beautiful paradox of the Christian calling: we are privileged and honored to be ambassadors for Christ, and at the same time, like the ass, we are humble servants.

The day I spent in Canchais was a *crosspoint* for me. I had never thought of myself as an ass before (except maybe when I've made a fool of myself!). The word has taken on new meaning for me, and when I hear it, I am drawn both to the mission in Canchias and to Christ's entry into Jerusalem.

May I, too, be as an ass, ready for humble service when Christ has need of me.

Jet Lag

*I*n November 2000, I flew to Africa and had my first experience of jet lag. Never having traveled so far before, I didn't quite know what to expect. I was traveling with a large group of Ambassadors for Children volunteers, all of us destined for Nairobi, Kenya where we would be involved in several different mission projects. In addition to the mission work, we were also scheduled to go on safari in the Masai Mara. For the first several nights, I woke up around 3:00 a.m., ready to go! I would barely get back to sleep before it was time to get up, eat breakfast, and head out to our mission site. After arriving home, I fell asleep every night on the sofa and dragged myself to bed around 9:00 p.m.

I've been thinking about how jet lag is not just a physical condition. There is also an emotional or psychological "jet lag" in hopping back and forth between diverse cultures. While I thoroughly enjoy experiencing other cultures—the food, music, art, customs and people—I find it hard to wrap my mind around the reality of the disparity between my McQuick, disposable products-dependent society and the more laid back and less consumer-oriented culture of Africa. Not once did I stand in a fast food line or eat off paper, plastic or Styrofoam products while I was in Africa. I also struggle with the wealth and waste in my life in comparison to the poverty and resourcefulness of the poor who make up the majority of people on this planet.

Another aspect of "jet lag" is that my heart is torn between being home with those I love and being in Africa with the Kenyan people and places that are now a special part of my reality as well. Even though I'm glad to be home, I find myself longing to be back in Kenya where life is slower paced, where I was content to live in a tent (deluxe tent, complete with bathroom) and out of a suitcase, and where I can feed my soul on the beauty of God's creation among the creatures of the Masai Mara. And my body is not happy to be back in the cold!

There are many ways that we become "jet lagged." When we lose a job; when someone we love dies or we receive a disturbing medical diagnosis; when a spouse announces that they want a divorce; or when the police call to tell us there's been an accident or one of our children has been picked up for driving under the influence, there is a lag between the reality that we know and are comfortable with and the new reality that we now must deal with. Often we wait in the "terminal of denial" hoping for a flight that will take us back to where we came from, away from the problems we are facing. For a time, we may "fly away" into fantasies and wishful thinking, into destructive activities that numb our pain and distress.

Whatever the form "jet lag" takes in our lives, there are strategies and resources to help us make the transition: the support of loved ones, friends and professionals, such as a pastor or counselor; spiritual practices such as prayer and communal worship; journaling, support groups, exercising to relieve stress, making sure we are eating right and getting enough sleep; and granting ourselves and others the grace to make mistakes and to not have to do things perfectly.

There is One, however, who transcends all time zones, who dwells in the highest heavens and yet who is as close as your own heart. The reality of Christ—and the gift of salvation that He brings—overcomes all our jet lags.

I trust in your unfailing love;
my heart rejoices in your salvation.
Psalm 13:5 NIV

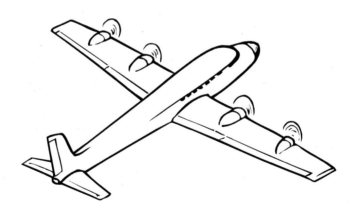

Stuck In the Mud

I waited patiently for the Lord; he turned to me and heard my cry.
He lifted me out of the slimy pit, out of the mud and mire;
he set my feet on a rock and gave me a firm place to stand.
Psalm 40:1-2 NIV

*N*ature-metaphor-lover that I am, I am extremely curious to know just what the psalmist's "slimy pit" experience was and how he got out of it.

Literally speaking, I have never found myself in a slimy pit and I hope I never do! The closest I've ever come was at our mission site in Nairobi, Kenya, a long awaited rain having transformed the school courtyard into a true suck-your-shoes-off mud pit. I had two close calls with "biting the mud," and if it hadn't been for someone reaching out and grabbing hold of me, or me clutching on to the only person within my reach, I would have been writing a drastically different story. I've never experienced anything quite so slippery, except maybe for ice. Perhaps enduring a stint in a slimy pit would be a good challenge on one of those "reality" TV shows.

Figuratively speaking, I think I can identify with the psalmist, and I bet you can, too. I looked up "mire" in the dictionary where one definition was "bog." I've often commented that I'm getting "bogged down," never giving a thought to the origin of this phrase. When things get complicated or difficult, we refer to the situation as "getting muddy" and if I'm "dazed and confused" (which I often am!), I'm "muddled." If I make it through a difficult situation, in spite of my mistakes and confusion, I've managed to "muddle through."

To stretch the analogy a bit further, when someone is not cooperating with our great idea, we might say that he or she is being "a stick-in-the-mud." Slanderous remarks are referred to as "mud-slinging" and a person who will stoop to just about anything is a "slime-ball." There are also those times in life when we feel like we are "in a rut." You've got to first have mud to make a rut! As we all know, getting out of a rut is not an easy task.

And what about all those times when things happen that don't seem fair or when we're feeling depressed and, in exasperation or discouragement, we utter, "It's the pits!"

If you've ever been accused of "wallowing in self-pity," or, worse yet, been told that "your name is mud," I bet you bristled that someone has the audacity to insinuate such a thing! Try calling someone a "pig" and you just might find yourself in the mud!

Obviously, I'm having a great time here playing in the mud. But what exactly is my point? My point is that life, more often than not, can be a muddy endeavor. Sometimes we create our own muddy mess and other times the mud is just there and unavoidable. Coming through and out of a muddy situation with "mud on your face" can be a very humbling experience.

The good news is that the Creator of dirt and water can pull us out of the muck and set us on a rock. Because of our Rescuer, we can stand firmly, mud and all.

"Gezundheit!"

Snot and Grace – Part II

*I*n May 2003, Rex and I traveled to Costa Rica where we were to meet up with our daughter, Beth, who had already spent ten weeks there student teaching at the Country Day School in Brazilito. The three of us were to participate in an eye care mission and we were excited about celebrating our 30th wedding anniversary in a tropical paradise. The fact that we would be able to combine a personal vacation with a mission trip was an added blessing.

While I was "out of the country," my "Pondering the Crosspoints," entitled "Snot and Grace," (see Chapter 5, page 74) was to appear in our church newsletter. I was a little bit anxious about the reception of this piece, anticipating a few "Oh my gosh!"es and "Well, I never!"s from the more conservative members of our congregation. Several times I thought I heard my ears ringing, but as it turns out, this physical phenomena was totally unrelated to the buzz I thought I was creating back home.

Before publishing "Snot and Grace," I sought, and received, the blessings of all the major players mentioned in the snotty scenarios. I spoke with my pastor, John Young, and received his blessing as well. Even so, I felt like I was climbing out on a limb and had invited him out there with me. I was an avid tree climber as a child, but over the years I've developed a fear of heights, and I did not relish a "fall from grace" among my peers. But up the tree I went! While perched together precariously on what felt like a very bouncy, flimsy limb, John spoke to my reservations: "Well, if anyone has difficulty with your writing, they just need an extra dose of grace." More grace-filled words I've never heard!

Evidently God was not finished with my "Lessons From Snot." Two days into our trip —on our thirtieth wedding anniversary, no less—my sinuses unleashed a flow of drainage for which there were not enough tissues in all of Costa Rica to contain. Tissues are a third-world luxury and, as a member of the "Kleenex Generation," I panicked when my supply from home quickly ran out. Having experienced a cold during her stay in Costa Rica, Beth tipped me off to the paper towel dispensers, which very few rest rooms provide (it's so HOT there that one's hands air dry before you can reach for the door knob).

The Costa Rican paper towels, thinner that what we use in the U.S, proved to be better snot-catchers than anything thus far developed by the combined efforts of Kleenex, Puffs, and Scotties! But, as I alluded to earlier, these heaven-sent dispensers of grace were few and far between, and I had to filch and hoard whatever I could of the valuable commodity whenever possible. I did find a few miniature boxes of actual "Kleenex" brand tissues strategically placed around one of our lodgings, but these pour excuses for tissues could not even handle the emission of one of my tender nostrils.

Now, I don't know about you, but I find uncontrollable fits of sneezing, coughing, and blowing my nose in public a bit embarrassing. Even though I know Emily Post would be aghast at my public display of nose control (Mom having taught me that it is impolite to blow one's nose at the dinner table), I was at the mercy of my out of control proboscis. If I had excused myself from the table every time I needed to clear my nostrils (doesn't that sound "politically correct"?), I would have missed entire meals at a time and missed the opportunity to get acquainted with many of the mission team members. Fortunately, my traveling companions looked on me with pity and accepted me, snot and all, with grace and aplomb.

It wasn't until I was back home that it occurred to me that God had given me my very own "snotty" lesson on grace. Once again, my fears of rejection—rooted in long ago childhood experiences—were proven false. Every day, several people would ask me how I was feeling and express empathy for my condition. Jeanine had gotten sick during our mission trip to Kenya in 2000, so she was especially compassionate and supportive. Tom, her husband, informed me that I could request a medical consult at the hotel desk. Jeanette's husband is susceptible to pneumonia, and she was so concerned about my cough, that she thought I should be Med-Jet-ted home. Nuria, our Coco de Playa Lion's Club hostess, took me to a farmacia for cough medicine (nasty tasting stuff—like what I imagine turpentine to taste like!). Bob gave me a supply of better tasting Americano cough syrup that went down much easier. And Rex and Beth were so loving and sweet. I couldn't have felt more loved and accepted.

While I wish I'd not been sick on our trip, between all the coughing fits, sneezes, and blowing, I did manage to enjoy being reunited with Beth, the beauty of God's prolific handiwork—Pacific sunsets, itsy-bitsy sand crabs scurrying on ocean beaches, exotic butterflies and birds vividly accenting the Cloud Forest, brilliant orange lava trickling down Mt. Arenal—and the companionship of many wonderful people. Once again, grace came through.

Ah... Ah... Ah... Excuse me... Ah... does anyone have... Ahhhhhhh... a tissue?????????????

The Lord bless you and keep you;
the Lord make his face shine upon you and be gracious to you;
the Lord turn his face toward you and give you—a tissue (peace).
Numbers 6:24-26 NIV

What Would Jesus Do?

Then the King will say to those on his right, "Come, you who are blessed by my
Father; take your inheritance, the kingdom prepared for you since the creation of
the world. For I was hungry and you gave me something to eat, I was thirsty and
you gave me something to drink, I was a stranger and you invited me in, I needed
clothes and you clothed me, I was sick and you looked after me, I was in prison and
you came to visit me." Then the righteous will answer him, "Lord, when did we see
you hungry and feed you, or thirsty and give you something to drink? When did
we see you a stranger and invite you in, or needing clothes and clothe you? When
did we see you sick or in prison and go to visit you?" The King will reply,
"I tell you the truth, whatever you did for one of the least of these
brothers of mine, you did for me."
Matthew 25:34-40 NIV

I stood surrounded by excited Honduran children, their brown, dirty arms extended
upward toward the plastic grocery bags of rice and beans I was carrying, bouncing
up and down, vying for my attention. One little boy, standing right in front of me
kept repeating, "Para mi mamá! Para mi mamá! (for my mama!)" My meager
supply of food was going quickly and I only had one more bag each of rice and
beans. I felt overwhelmed, and as I gave the last of my supplies away, I looked up
at a mother watching passively from the sidelines, and I felt sick.

What must it be like to struggle daily to find food to feed these hungry children?
What must it feel like to see food so close at hand, but not be one of the lucky
recipients? As I stood with my empty plastic grocery bags, I had to tell the children,
"No mas. (no more)" I don't think I've ever felt so awful as I did at that moment.
I offered my empty sacks to one little guy, knowing that even the sacks will be of
some use to someone who has lost everything in the wake of Hurricane Mitch. He
was deeply disappointed with my offering, but he took them and walked away.

I have this painful moment recorded on videotape and when I watch it, it doesn't
seem real. It feels like I'm watching a documentary film, yet I know that the woman
on the tape is me, experiencing the reality of a third world country. These children
are among the 2,000 people living around the edge of a soccer stadium in make-shift
dwellings formed out of blankets, sheets of plastic, and cardboard that were salvaged
from the wreckage of Hurricane Mitch and the aftermath of flooding. These people
have no homes to go home to.

Walking back into my lovely, spacious home on cozy Wayside Lane was difficult and the image of the hungry, homeless children in Honduras does not fade quickly. I find myself asking, "What would Jesus do?" Well, he would take five loaves and two fishes and turn them into a picnic feast! Given my lack of miraculous touch, what are my options? My friends try to encourage me by saying, "But you did so much on your mission trip!" Yes, we provided a valuable service of vision care to 4500 people—a wonderful accomplishment. Yet in the midst of so much need and poverty, it seems like such a drop in the bucket.

Perhaps what Jesus would have me do is share my discomfort and concern with others, in the hopes that we will all be more grateful for what we have, more sensitive to the needs of others around the world, and more likely to forego some of our luxuries, give some of our own time, to help those less fortunate.

I wrote the above essay in March 1999, and seven and a half years later, my stomach knots and my eyes sting with tears as I read and relive this story: the look of disappointment and frustration in the little boy's eyes; the impassive eyes of the mother observing the children begging for food; the anger and helplessness I felt when I had no food left to give out… I think also about how easy it has become to turn a blind eye and return to my life of privilege.

Following my first few mission trips, my re-entry had me feeling like I had one foot planted in the U.S. and one planted in Honduras, with two different videos of my life playing in my head. It was hard to feel present, to re-engage in life as usual, to shake off the reality of the poverty that characterizes so much of the world.

Then one year, I returned home and hit the deck running, realizing only days later that my re-entry had been significantly different. I was shocked that I could so quickly and easily put Honduras out of sight, out of mind. My thoughts drift toward Honduras frequently—daily even, and I always look forward to the next trip with growing anticipation. But it disturbs me that I seem to have reconciled my privilege with the poverty of others.

I'm not sure if this is a good thing or a bad thing. Perhaps it is some of both…

Exiled

This is what the Lord Almighty, the God of Israel, says to all those
I carried into exile from Jerusalem to Babylon: "Build houses and
settle down; plant gardens and eat what they produce. Marry and have sons and
daughters; find wives for your sons and give your daughters in marriage, so that
they too may have sons and daughters. Increase in number there; do not
decrease. Also, seek the peace and prosperity of the city to which
I have carried you into exile. Pray to the Lord for it, because if
it prospers, you too will prosper."
Jeremiah 29:4-7 NIV

I have never been exiled from my country, thus, in pondering the relevance of this
passage for my life, I look for a metaphorical message from the prophet Jeremiah.
How have I been "carried into exile"? The closest I can come to understanding exile
is my experience when our first baby, Jason, died when only a few hours old.
As a grieving mother, I remember writing about feeling as if I had turned a corner
and was suddenly, unexplainably in a foreign world—like being in a nightmare from
which I could not wake up. In many ways this new territory looked much the same,
populated by the same people, places, tasks, of my familiar life. Yet deep within me,
I had been torn from one reality and placed in a parallel reality and the feeling was
not pleasant! How could I then—and how can any of us—"build houses and settle
down" in the awful emotional places we find ourselves when loved ones die, jobs are
downsized, cancer is confirmed, divorce is announced?

*"When seventy years are completed for Babylon, I will come to you
and fulfill my gracious promise to bring you back to this place.
For I know the plans I have for you," declares the Lord,
"plans to prosper you and not to harm you, plans to give you hope and a future.
Then you will call upon me and come and pray to me, and I will listen to you.
You will seek me and find me when you seek me with all your heart.
I will be found by you," declares the Lord, "and will bring you back from captivity."
Jeremiah 29:10-14 NIV*

The message I draw from Jeremiah is not that we should resign ourselves to our exiled state—give up, give in—which is an understandable place we visit as we adjust to our unwelcome condition; but rather, that we continue to live life with hope, knowing that God has not abandoned us, will come for us, wants us to seek him with all our hearts—and find God's loving presence, even in the midst of exile.

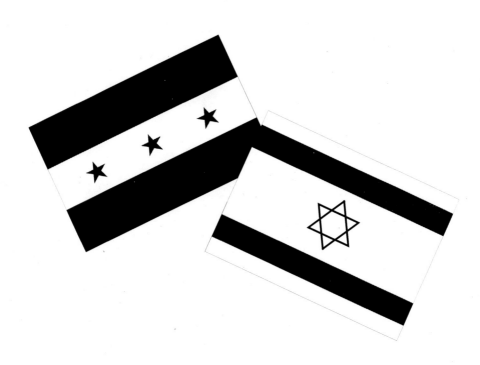

Chapter VII

Women of Grace

Charm is deceptive, and beauty is fleeting;
but a woman who fears the Lord is to be praised.
Proverbs 31:30 NIV

Well behaved women seldom make history.
~ Laurel Thatcher Ulrich[43]

I'm not afraid of storms, for I'm learning to sail my ship.
~ Louisa May Alcott

43 Ulrich, Laurel Thatcher, "Virtuous Women Found: New England Ministerial Literature, 1668-1735,"
American Quarterly 28 (1976): 20.

A Letter From Christ

You yourselves are our letter, written on our hearts, known and read by everybody. You show that you are a letter from Christ, the result of our ministry, written not with ink but with the Spirit of the living God, not on tablets of stone but on tablets of human hearts.
2 Corinthians 3:2-3 NIV

*W*hen I was a child, I attended Martin Luther Elementary School in Buffalo, New York, and during my second and third grade years, I had the most wonderful teacher. Miss Albers was the prettiest, smartest, kindest, most fun teacher ever created! Midway through my third grade year, my family moved to Indiana and I had to say goodbye to Miss Albers. My parents were fond of my teacher, as well, and I was delighted that they kept in touch with her. I was so excited when the news came that she was to be married and that she and her husband were to be missionaries in New Guinea. I have a picture of the happy couple with their baby girl, Debra, and a second picture of their two little girls sitting on a blanket with grass huts in the background. Miss Albers was now more wonderful that ever—and I wanted to be "just like her" when I grew up!

Could it be that the seed for missions was written on my heart, so many years ago, by the example of a woman who created a safe, warm, nurturing environment in which to learn and grow? I think St. Paul would say a resounding "Yes! Yes, indeed!" I am your letter, Miss Albers, and because of you, the Spirit of the living God is written on my heart.

C. S. Lewis, one of my favorite writers, had a great deal to say about love and vulnerability. I believe that we all come into this world with tender hearts vulnerable to the touch of the Spirit, open to the love of God. When someone like Miss Albers writes upon our hearts, we learn to be open and vulnerable, willing to risk love.

However, when someone with a wounded heart, wields the pen of rejection, criticism, and discouragement, our hearts become hardened lest we be hurt again. Most of us have experienced both kinds of etchings, and a battle ensues within: Should I reach out, risk, be vulnerable? Should I withdraw and protect myself from hurt?

I am very thankful for Miss Albers, as well as the many other wonderful people, who have written upon my heart with the Spirit of the living God. I am their letter. I, too, have written upon the vulnerable hearts of many individuals, and they are my letter. I pray that, more times than not, it is God's Spirit who guides my pen, yet all too often I flinch with shame for a wounding mark I have carelessly left. It is an awesome privilege and responsibility—and an amazing gift of grace—to be both the pen of Grace *and* the tablet upon which Grace is written.

Lamplight

Ten virgins...went out to meet the bridegroom. Five of them were foolish and five were wise. The foolish ones took their lamps but did not take any oil with them.

Matthew 25:1-3 NIV

*A*mong the most difficult *crosspoints* in life are those that are unexpected: a spouse or parent has a sudden heart attack; a mammogram reveals something suspicious; a trusted spouse has an affair; downsizing at the plant eliminates a "secure" job; a much wanted pregnancy abruptly ends due to miscarriage; a newly licensed adolescent loses control of her car on the way home from work at a fast food restaurant on a moonless, rainy evening...

Like the women in Matthew 25, who set out to meet the bridegroom with only their lamps, we often find ourselves unprepared for the unexpected arrival of pain and suffering—and even joyful surprises. What is the "oil" missing from our lamps when crisis forces us to take an unfamiliar and scary detour or when opportunity knocks and new doors open for us? What "lamps" do we foolishly put our faith in, neglecting to secure the Oil to keep them burning: Money? Status? Education? Friends in high places? Health and life insurance? Tenure? What fuels *you* as you journey through the *crosspoints* of life?

What good are our lamps without the Oil?

"Grace Means Gift"

Minnie Schelesky Reuman
1887-1972

A few years ago, my mom gave me her most prized possession—her mother's Bible. It's small, by today's standards, with tiny print, bound in a leather cover—the King James Version, of course.

What I treasure most about this Bible is my Grandmother's written notes. My own Bible has many passages highlighted and underlined, with comments written in the margin, the really good pages dog-earred. So it was with great interest that I opened Grandma's Bible to see what passages were most dear to her. I was disappointed to discover that she had only written one small comment—but it is a comment that speaks volumes.

In very tiny cursive, at the top of the "Presented to" page, Grandma wrote "grace means gift." That's it. Grace means gift. After my initial disappointment, my heart swelled with the realization that this one tiny phrase was the heart of my grandmother's heart. At the time I discovered her note, I was in the midst of my own discovery of God's grace. I'm always amazed (but not surprised) at God's impeccable timing. If I had read Grandma's comment a couple years earlier, would it have had the same impact? I think not. God saved this precious discovery for a time when I would be most able to receive the full impact of its blessing.

Grandma's legacy—the realization of God's amazing grace—was passed down to me through my mother. I'm not referring here to Mom handing over Grandma's Bible to me, but to her own faith journey and personal encounters with "grace means gift." Every time she tells me her own story of discovering grace, her face glows and her voice takes on the quality of music—an expression that makes me say to myself, "I want that! I want to have what she has!"

Mom grew up in Attica, New York, a quiet little village that unfortunately became famous for the horrible prison uprising of September 1971. As a child, she attended a small United Brethren Church. After marrying my dad—an Irish Catholic (with a touch of English thrown in for polish)—they gravitated to the Lutheran denomination, which proved to be a nice compromise for their very different faith traditions. God placed them within walking distance of Bethany Lutheran Church, which became the church of my early childhood.

Lutheranism introduced Mom to Martin Luther and his heart-shaking discovery of grace: "For by grace you have been saved through faith, and that not of yourself; it is the gift of God" (Ephesians 2:8 NIV). Luther's revelation of God's grace transformed his relationship with God from one in which he believed that he had to earn God's favor and pay for his transgressions, to a seemingly almost-too-good-to-be-true, grace-filled relationship. His discovery paved the way for the birth of the Protestant church.

Even though my mom was raised in the church, it wasn't until she was 59 that she really "got" grace. Mom recently wrote and published her autobiography—a priceless gift to her grandchildren—and in it she states, "Unknowingly, there had been a struggle in my life as I wavered back and forth for many years, trying to earn my own salvation FOR God, instead of accepting it as a free gift FROM God through Christ!."

Each one of us has to experience our very own encounter with grace. Grace is such a difficult concept to grasp. Being raised in the church by godly parents isn't our ticket into the realm of grace. But once we've "got" grace, we want to share it. And it is through demonstrating grace toward others that we help them "get" grace.

We can lead our spouse, children and friends to the water trough of grace, but they have to taste it for themselves in order to experience its refreshing, life sustaining truth. Often times, we arrive at the water trough via trauma, crisis, loss, grief—literally dying of thirst, spiritually. Care for a sip?

"Grandma's legacy—the realization of God's amazing grace—was passed down to me through my mother."

A Dangerous Woman

"...let us encourage one another."
Hebrews 10:25 NIV

I want to be "a dangerous woman." Yes, that's right. A dangerous woman. Before I explain, let me ask you a trivia question: During World War II, who did Adolf Hitler dub "the most dangerous woman in Europe"? Need a few hints? It was someone who bore a crown and a title to go with it; someone who would never go out in public without her hat and gloves and a pocketbook on her arm. If you guessed Queen Elizabeth (mother of the current Queen of England), then you may go to the head of the class.

I came across this tidbit of world history while listening to a Patsy Clairmont tape in my car. According to Patsy, following the air raids on London, Queen Elizabeth would go out into the streets to offer encouragement to her frightened subjects. She also chose not to send her own children away from the city because many of her subjects were not financially able to provide such safety for their children. I don't know if this is the sole or main reason Hitler feared this courageous, caring, pocketbook-packing-parent, but it does make me ponder the power of encouragement.

As a therapist, I continually offer encouragement to my clients. It's easy to be an encourager when it's not my crisis. But what about when I find myself in crisis? In Romans 1:12, Paul instructs us to mutually encourage each other with our faith. I've not experienced many serious crises, but when I have, I tend to be self-absorbed in my own problems.

I remember back a few years to the ice storm that left many of us without power for several days. My main focus was on staying warm! No way was I going to venture out into the cold! Granted, residents were told to stay home until the danger of downed power lines and falling tree limbs was taken care of, but surely there was something I could have done besides follow the sunbeams from room to room wrapped in my sleeping bag…

To rise above crisis and self requires self-discipline, empathy, love, compassion, courage—and faith. Faith that in the midst of crisis, God is present. Such qualities are "dangerous" because they have the power to transform, empower, and encourage others to tap their own inner reservoirs of God-given strengths.

To be fair to myself, there have been times when I've risen to the occasion, in the midst of crisis, and been a "Queen Elizabeth." In those moments, I can feel the empowering Spirit and I am aware of how little of "me" and how much of "Spirit" is at work.

Sometimes it's the littlest things, those seemingly minuscule, "Oh, it was nothing!" acts of kindness that pack the power to energize and inspire or to bring peace and comfort. Each and every one of us can be a Queen Elizabeth each and every day. Hat, gloves and pocketbook not required!

Chapter VIII

Through the Eyes of a Child

Jesus said,
"I tell you the truth, unless you change
and become like little children, you
will never enter the kingdom of heaven."
Matthew 18:2-4 NIV

This Little Boy
(For Matthew)

This little boy with eyes of blue,
Who stole my heart when he was new;
Now stands and gazes down at me,
Who once came only to my knee.

This little boy with curious heart,
Who frazzled me (it was his art!),
Now calmly sits and contemplates
Maturity, on which he waits.

This little boy with hugs galore,
Whose fleeting kiss made my heart soar;
Now shuns a motherly embrace;
Delivers no more hearts with lace.

This little boy of energy,
Who climbed all things as if a tree;
Now concentrates his powers that be,
Discovering truths in all he sees.

This little boy who stole my heart,
With whom reluctantly I part;
Now carries off a mother's tear,
But memories will hold him near.

The Spirituality of Wonder

O Lord, you have searched me and you know me.
You know when I sit and when I rise; you perceive my thoughts from afar. You
discern my going out and my lying down; you are familiar with all my ways. Before
a word is on my tongue you know it completely, O Lord. You hem me in—behind
and before; you have laid your hand upon me. Such knowledge is
too wonderful for me, too lofty for me to attain.
Psalm 139:1-6 NIV

*W*hen you are in a wondering mood, what captures your wonderment? Can you recall the last time you were enthralled by the mystery of grace? As adults, we've little time in our busy lives to stop and indulge in childlike wonder. Sadly, like an unused muscle, this precious, life-giving ability seems to atrophy.

Recently I sat in wonder as I held my neighbors' new baby daughter. And little Johnna gazed in wonder at—everything! For her, the world is fresh and captivating, just as it was for Adam and Eve when they opened their eyes for the first time in the Garden of Eden.

We are surrounded by the wonder of God's creative frenzy, yet somehow we often see right past it. Bouts of fear, worry, resentment, complaining, lethargy, grief, anger, sadness, _____ (you fill in the blank) cloud our vision. The challenges of life, and the emotions they unleash, are *crosspoints* on which we teeter between growth and retreat.

Often it is in the very midst of a crisis that we encounter God's living presence in life-changing ways. Brennan Manning, states that "the spirituality of wonder knows the world is charged with grace, that while sin and war, disease and death are terribly real, God's loving presence and power in our midst are even more real."[44]

Recognizing a subtle, spine-tingling charge of grace, and responding with wonder, is sometimes even more elusive as we deal with the ordinary, mundane activities of daily life. For me, little children, furry animals, and nature are gifts of grace that, in the words of Joy Sawyer, "help me return to the sense of wonder at common, everyday events."[45]

---

44 Maning, Brennan, The Ragamuffin Gospel, Multnomah Publishers, 2000, p. 98.
45 Saywer, Joy, Dancing to the Heartbeat of Redemption, InterVarsity Press, 2000.

Little children are enthralled with the itty-bitty. When my daughter, Beth, was a tot, the sight of a daddy-longlegs was cause for excited squeals and uncontrollable bouncing, and all action came to an abrupt halt while she paused in rapt attention, fully absorbed in her latest discovery. Then would come the non-stop questions about every minute aspect of the newly discovered creature. And this process would be repeated *with each-and-every* daddy-longlegs she spied—every day—*for an entire summer*! A child's wonder can be exhausting for a busy toddler's parent!

Our heavenly parent welcomes our questions and delights in our curiosity and is never exhausted by our wonder. Whether you are in the midst of an overwhelming crisis or trudging through the tedium and frustrations of an ordinary day, I pray that you will have the eyes of an infant, the curiosity of a child, and the attentiveness of the psalmist, discovering anew a "world charged with grace."

My Little Chickadee

Holy Father, protect them by the power of your name—the
name you gave me—so they may be one as we are one...
My prayer is not that you take them out of the world but
that you protect them from the evil one.
John 17:11, 15 NIV

*W*hile contemplating Jesus' prayer for the protection of his disciples, I remembered something I wrote years ago about God's protection:

"Mom! Mom! Do 'ya know how a bird can sleep on a tree branch an' not fall off?" my preschooler shouted breathlessly as he raced in from school one day. To be quite honest, this was not a question I'd ever pondered, but once it was drawn to my attention, my curiosity was piqued. In my mind, I envisioned a Carolina Chickadee bobbing in the wind, securely attached to a barren wintry branch of my tulip tree. It is indeed amazing how a little bird can do this!

According to my son, Matt, the budding ornithologist, as a bird relaxes, its claws respond by tightening securely around the branch. I found myself fascinated by this fact and enjoyed a renewed appreciation for the tender creativity evident in God's design for caring for His precious creatures.

We, too, need to relax in His loving care and find ourselves securely attached to the Vine. In the letting go of worries, outcomes, and other people, we find strength to withstand the gusts of life. We can rest in safety knowing God is awake and ever in control.

You alone, O Lord, make me dwell in safety.
Psalm 4:8 NIV

Jellybeans [45]

Ask and you will receive, and your joy will be complete.
John 16:24 NIV

*O*ne day when I was about five, my brother, Michael, and I accompanied our mother on a visit to the home of a woman I did not know. A seemingly insignificant event occurred that day that served as a powerful metaphor for the way I would approach life for many years.

Our hostess welcomed my brother and me by offering us an opportunity to reach into a glass jar laden with colorful, shiny jellybeans. Being a girl, I was given the first chance. Timidly I stuck my little hand into the tempting jar and carefully removed one jellybean. I stood in amazement and despair as my brother brazenly reached deep into the jar and captured a fistful of jellybeans. It had not occurred to me that I could have more than one, nor could I bring myself to ask for a second helping, even after observing my brother's audacious display.

As I look back on my life, I can see how I have embraced many God-given opportunities in a similar fashion. It has always been hard for me to ask for what I need, let alone what I want. Even when God places an opportunity in my path, God usually has to provide an encourager to convince me that it's mine to take. Over time, I've grown to realize that I am indeed "worthy" to receive God's blessings; worthy—by the grace of God.

What "jellybean" do you not feel worthy of?

---

46 Teeple, Linda, originally published as "I Am Worthy," <u>Voices of Hope: Daily Meditations for Persons In Recovery</u>, Caroline Smith, Ed., Warner Press.

Aardvarks and Eyeglasses

Jesus said,
"Let the little children come to me, and do not hinder them,
for the kingdom of God belongs to such as these. I tell you the truth,
anyone who will not receive the kingdom of God
like a little child, will never enter it."
And he took the children in his arms,
put his hands on them and blessed them.
Mark 10:14-16 NIV

I learn something new every time I'm with my little friend, Hannah, a precocious, bubbling fountain of new discoveries and fresh perspectives. Several years ago, when she was four, we met my husband for lunch (a few bites of macaroni and applesauce, and *lots* of coloring) and then Hannah and I went to the library. Hannah set right to the task of selecting book after book. "We'll need a B-I-G sack today!" she exclaimed later as we checked out a towering stack of glossy covered books at the circulation desk.

One of Hannah's selections was about Arthur Aardvark getting eyeglasses. "I wonder if Arthur goes to the same eye doctor that you do?" I asked. It just so happens that my husband is Hannah's optometrist. Hannah pondered my question briefly and then informed me that, no, Arthur would go to Steve. Puzzled, I initially guessed that maybe Steve was another character in the book. Then it suddenly occurred to me that Hannah was probably referring to her uncle. Before I could check this out, Hannah chattered on about her uncle, the vet-er-i-nar-i-an, pronouncing the term perfectly.

"Of course," I thought. "Animals don't go to people doctors!" Amazed at Hannah's knowledge, it took a few seconds for me to realize that I, the adult, was thinking like a child and Hannah, the child, was thinking like an adult. Using my imagination, I pictured the personified aardvark going to a people doctor. Hannah, on the other hand, slipping out of her imagination and into logical thinking, deduced that the aardvark, being an animal, would go to an animal doctor. Later, Hannah's mother, Sandra, laughed delightedly as I shared this story of her daughter's precocity with her.

Jesus said that we must become like a little child in order to enter the Kingdom of Heaven. Untainted by the harshness of life, their minds open, innocent and trusting, children are able to imagine and embrace a God of love and grace. The reality of God for a child is an open book, clean, crisp pages awaiting the imprinting of life's experiences that speak of God's presence. What are we teaching our children about God—and what would we do well to learn from our children about entering into relationship with God?

> *But seek ye first the kingdom of God, and his righteousness;*
> *and all these things shall be added unto you.*
> *Matthew 6:33 KJV*

Liberty and Grace

"The Spirit of the Lord is on me because he has anointed me...
to proclaim freedom for the prisoners...
to release the oppressed."
Luke 4:18 NIV

"I pledge allegiance, to the flag..." recites the shy little girl, with amazing ease and confidence for one so young. She is standing beside her school desk dressed in a wrinkled, white, cotton blouse, a pleated plaid skirt hanging slightly askew, knee socks at their usual half mast on her skinny, flag pole legs, her scuffed saddle shoes toed inward. With her tiny, right hand positioned over her heart, her energetic body wiggling and squirming (as are all the other second graders' bodies), she solemnly faces the flag and recites the Pledge of Allegiance flawlessly. She is proud—so proud—that she knows e-v-e-r-y single word by heart, right down to a lustily proclaimed, *"...with liberty and justice for all."*

That little girl was me, when I was seven. The true meaning of this pledge was way over my head back then, but over the years, the Pledge of Allegiance has taken on deeper meaning.

Given that I am a citizen of a great democratic republic that strives to provide "liberty and justice for all," I think I know what liberty is. But, in truth, how can I really know the meaning of liberty if I have never been without it?

I grew up *white* through the civil rights movement. I came of age *female* in the 70's and the Women's Movement. I have been blessed to be a *mother* in a land where children are valued (well-fed, clothed, sheltered, immunized, educated...). Not once have I been refused entrance to a restaurant due to the shade of my skin. Never have I been denied education or beaten at whim because of my gender, as continues to be the case in some countries, for example, in the Middle East. Nor have I ever been persecuted for being a Christian or for expressing my opinion or asking questions. No, I can't even begin to imagine what it must be like to have my freedom taken away or to have *never* known liberty. I have a strong sense of entitlement when it comes to my civil liberties and I glibly take my freedom for granted. I don't like admitting this—but it's true.

Jesus declared, "The Spirit of the LORD is upon Me, because He has anointed Me…to proclaim liberty to the captives…to set at liberty those who are oppressed" (Luke 4:18 NKJV). My precious Savior—the living, breathing grace of God—liberated me spiritually. My ancestors came to America in search of freedom and opportunity. My father and all my uncles fought in WWII to preserve our freedom here in America and to bring liberation around the globe. What can *I* do to follow in the footsteps of my liberators?

I detest war and grieve the casualties (such a benign, "casual" word for the people who have been wounded, taken captive as POWs, or lost their lives or loved ones). Hearing the stories of the atrocities perpetrated against the Iraqi people, by their own government, and witnessing the saga of the Iraqi war, drives home to me *my* responsibility to find ways to be a liberator, like Christ and the brave men and women who died to set and keep me free.

While I won't be marching into battle any time soon, as a marriage and family therapist, I am witness to many bitter skirmishes and war torn families, so I have ample opportunity to bring aid to the front lines.

How might God be calling you to serve in his "coalition of the willing"? Where are the front lines in your life? What might you do to "proclaim liberty to the captives," and "set at liberty those who are oppressed"? We can be held captive in many ways. For example, survivors of abuse are often oppressed by shame, fear, and low self esteem, and held hostage for years by trauma from the past.

When we observe the 4th of July, let's be mindful of how very blessed we are to live in "the land of the free" and look for opportunities to bring hope and liberation to the captives in our midst. For "where the Spirit of the Lord is, there is liberty" (2 Corinthians 3:17 NKJV).

Chapter IX

Snakes and Snails and Puppy Dog Tales

All things bright and beautiful,
all creatures great and small,
All things wise and wonderful,
the Lord God made them all.
~ *Cecil Humphreys*[47]

Bring into the ark two of all living creatures…
two of every kind of bird, of every kind of animal and of
every kind of creature that moves along the ground.
Genesis 6:19-20 NIV

The world's great age begins anew,
The Golden years return,
The earth doth like a snake renew
Her winter weeds outworn.
~ *Percy Bysshe Shelley*[48]

The dog was created specially for chidren.
He is the god of frolic.
~ *Henry Ward Beecher*[49]

---

47 Cecil Humphreys (1818-1895), Irish poetess and author, wrote "All Things Bright and Beautiful" in 1848 to amplify and simplify the first of the twelve clauses of the Apostles Creed.

48 Percy Bysshe Shelley, English Romantic poet, 1792-1822.

49 Henry Ward Beecher, clergyman, author, reformer and brother of Harriet Beecher Stowe (author of Uncle Tom's Cabin), 1813-1887.

SNAKE!

Be as shrewd as snakes and as innocent as doves.
Matthew 10:16 NIV

I am not fond of snakes. That's an understatement, to say the least. I detest them. They give me the weebie-jeebies. They make my skin crawl. I wouldn't touch one with a ten foot pole! I don't know—maybe it's something in my genes passed down to me from Eve to abhor snakes and screech at the sight of them.

So, of course, I marry a snake lover! Rex was a Steve Irwin-Jeff Corwin[50] type kid who picked up anything that moved and brought it home to become one of the family. Among his menagerie of legless reptiles were Slinky, a garter snake—*and* her twenty-four babies (another snake came for a visit with Slinky, and while there, engaged in a little hanky-panky and, alas, ended up being eaten by Slinky. "That Slinky—she was like that..." reports Rex); a rat snake that got run over by a car (while on loan to a friend), a blue racer who paid a show-and-tell visit to a biology class (and ended up being dissected)... (Are you seeing a pattern here?)

When we got married, our prenuptial agreement included two items: one, Rex requested that I keep him supplied with home baked cookies (and this from a girl who grew up believing cookies came packaged, ready to eat, from a store), and two, I requested—demanded, actually—that there never be *any* snakes in our home. Rex has abided by my request, and I abided by his up until we were both diagnosed with high cholesterol.

Rex and I both love the out-of-doors, but my adoration has its limits. I do not like to tent camp in the rain, or when the temperature dips to freezing (as it did the year we camped in Yellowstone National Park); I do not like to itch, sweat, or have surprise encounters with snakes, or any critter that might eat me. We took a lot of outdoorsy type vacations when the kids were little, one of which took us to Manitoulin Island in Lake Huron. One day when we were hiking in a dried up creek bed, three-year-old Beth's attention was captured by a flash of movement in the rocky bank.

---

50 Animal Planet naturalists and stars of "The Crocodile Hunter" and "Corwin's Quest."

"It's alive!" she stammered, in a quavering voice.

"Something in there is a-l-i-v-e!"

Adventurous Dad began pulling out rocks and tossing them aside, and much to his delight, he found a big black snake. I reacted by swiftly backtracking the way we'd come, and then, coming to my senses, ran back, scooped up Beth, and took off. As it turned out, Mr. Big-Black-Snake turned out to be harmless. "Crikey! What a beauty! Isn't she gorgeous? Woo-hooo!"

While I still think my collective unconscious is warning me that women and snakes do not mix, I no longer screech when a garter snake crosses my path, and I've even been known to touch—and even hold—one (but not without feeling as if snakes are slithering around in my shirt). Rex and the Animal Planet gang have helped me evolve in my understanding and appreciation of asps.

Wondering what the Bible might have to say about snakes, I did a search. From Genesis to Revelation, I found only one verse in which there is a positive reference to snakes. In Matthew 10:16, Jesus advises his disciples to "be as shrewd as snakes and as innocent as doves." Be like a snake? I think not! Be shrewd *and* innocent? Is this even possible? That Jesus—always wanting me to leave my comfort zone! And just when I'm starting to get comfortable!

Crocodile Christ

*O*ne of my favorite TV shows is "The Crocodile Hunter," featuring Aussie naturalist, Steve Irwin. There is no one I know of who is quite so enthusiastic about their job as Steve is. He's been an animal lover since he was a child, and as an adult, he acts just like a big, crazy, hyperactive kid. At first he was a little hard for me to stomach, his enthusiasm seemed so exaggerated and put on. But slowly I got hooked and have grown to love his antics, his passion for nature, and his good heart.

Countless times I have sat enthralled in front of my TV watching as Steve Erwin captures a crocodile, usually because it is ill and in need of medical attention or because its habitat is no longer suitable. The crocodile is always cranky and most uncooperative, unable to recognize and appreciate the kindness Steve is paying him. By the time the crocodile has been wrestled into submission, his body held down by five or six strong men, jaws held shut by Steve, and a canvas bag over its eyes, Steve is wet, muddy, breathless, tired, pumped and jubilant. There's nothing better than a good wrestling match with a feisty croc – except maybe a thrilling standoff with an extremely venomous snake! "Crikey!" declares Steve. " Isn't he the most gorgeous creature you've ever laid eyes on???!!!"

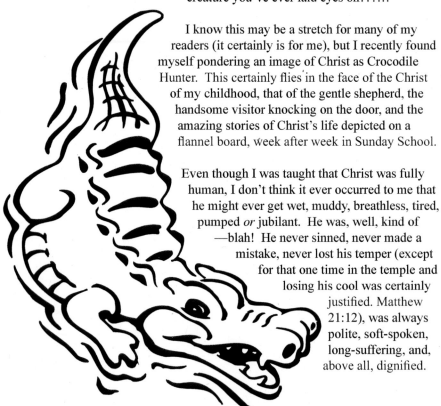

I know this may be a stretch for many of my readers (it certainly is for me), but I recently found myself pondering an image of Christ as Crocodile Hunter. This certainly flies in the face of the Christ of my childhood, that of the gentle shepherd, the handsome visitor knocking on the door, and the amazing stories of Christ's life depicted on a flannel board, week after week in Sunday School.

Even though I was taught that Christ was fully human, I don't think it ever occurred to me that he might ever get wet, muddy, breathless, tired, pumped *or* jubilant. He was, well, kind of —blah! He never sinned, never made a mistake, never lost his temper (except for that one time in the temple and losing his cool was certainly justified. Matthew 21:12), was always polite, soft-spoken, long-suffering, and, above all, dignified.

This new image of Crocodile Christ has invited me to see and experience Christ in an entirely new and refreshing way. To think that Christ would get wet and muddy for me when I wander into an unhealthy or dangerous habitat, wrestle me away from my worries, heartaches, fears, and bad habits, wear himself out rescuing me in spite of my rebellion and ungratefulness, and, surging with adrenaline, leap with joy and shout, "Crikey! Isn't she the most gorgeous creature you've ever laid eyes on???!!!"

I realize that Christ has done so much more for me than this image of Crocodile Christ can portray. While daring and brave, Steve, the Crocodile Hunter, does not knowingly wade out into crocodile-infested waters with the intent of giving his life for the crocodile. Oh, he often gets bruised and bloody, and takes what most of us consider rash, idiotic risks, but he definitely plans on surviving the adventure to tell about it.

For me, this colorful image of a zany Christ who is so crazy about me and so recklessly passionate about my welfare, that he willingly—and daily—plunges enthusiastically into crocodile-infested waters on my behalf, serves as a stepping stone in helping me grow toward being able to understand the miracle of Christ:

"While we were still sinners, Christ died for us."
Romans 5:8 NIV

"Christ has died; Christ has risen; Christ will come again."[51]

While I believe and claim this, I know that it is humanly impossible to truly and completely comprehend it. Amazingly, just a smidgen more of who Christ is has been revealed to me through the humanness of someone who, of all things, loves crocodiles.

I wrote "Crocodile Christ" in 2002 for my church newsletter column, "Pondering the Crosspoints." When Steve Irwin died on September 4—ten days ago—I was shocked and deeply saddened. With publication of this book only weeks away, I pondered whether or not to include "Crocodile Christ." I love this image of a zany, crazy-about-me Christ, and my heart's desire is to share it with others. Thus, I decided to keep it in as a tribute to this very special person who inspired the metaphor of Christ as crocodile hunter.

My ventures into nature rarely take me out of the woods behind my house, so I've enjoyed living vicariously through Steve. The world has lost a great naturalist, educator, environmentalist, and advocate of endangered animals and habitats, but Steve's legacy—his spirit, passion, and zest for life—will live on through those whose lives he's touched. Steve Irwin, Crocodile Hunter, has left his unique and indelible imprint on my heart and in my life.

"Crikey! I'm sure gonna' miss ya, mate!"

51 From A Service of Word and Table I (c)1972,1980,1985, 1989 The United Methodist Publishing House.

Lion of Judah

Do not weep! See, the Lion of the tribe of Judah,
the Root of David, has triumphed.
Revelation 5:5 NIV

Annie Dilliard, one of my favorite writers, thinks God is a madman and strongly advises us to don crash helmets before entering church. Describing the Biblical Lion of Judah, she pictures him as wild-maned. He cannot be tamed--nor chained.[52] And Joy Sawyer, while contemplating a "lifelong spiritual safari," speaks of a "woolly, holy wonder" that "roars around every corner."[53]

I don't know about you, but for me the image of Jesus as a roaring, wild-maned lion is quite intimidating and less than inviting. It's also hard to reconcile with my long-time favorite image of Jesus as Shepherd. Of course, there is that passage in the Bible that predicts a time when the lion will lay down with the lamb – a popular Christmas card picture – but this is really hard for me to cuddle up to. It's beyond my comprehension and experience.

Many years ago, my good friend, Lea, who was studying to be an elementary teacher, and avidly devouring children's literature, introduced me to The Chronicles of Narnia by C.S. Lewis. The "mane" character, Aslan, is an inhabitant of Narnia, an unseen world penetrable only to innocent, imaginative children whose hearts are open to mystery. This delightful fantasy, enjoyed equally by children and adults alike, is rich with spiritual metaphor. The saga of the children's experiences in Narnia parallels our own "spiritual safari" and relationship with Christ, the Lion of Judah.

I read Narnia before having children and loved it for its wonderful characters and adventure-filled story, as well as for the spiritual message encoded in its imagery. And I have since read it to both of my children when they were young. I think I need to read it again before I put on my crash helmet and go on safari with this madman Annie Dilliard speaks of!

---

52 Dillard, Annie, referenced in Dancing to the Heartbeat of Redemption, by Joy Sawyer, InterVarsity Press, 2000, p. 153.
53 Sawyer, Joy, Dancing to the Heartbeat of Redemption, InterVarsity Press, 2000, p. 153.

While I can't remember much of the story line and few of the names of the characters, I do remember the feeling of safety and security that grew in me as I journeyed through Narnia. It was a spiritual safari deeper than I've ever traveled into the tangled jungle of trust and faith. Aslan was powerful and scary, but also gentle and loving. My encounter with Aslan, if only as reader and voyeur, nurtured my trust in God, and I wanted my children to know Aslan as a door into understanding God.

I invite you to strap on your crash helmets and venture, however tentatively, into the jungle with a wild-maned madman. I imagine Jesus, the master of metaphor and parable, a broad smile stretched across his face and a twinkle in his eye, exclaiming,

"Now, why didn't *I* think of that one!"

The Lap of Grace

Come to me, all you who are weary and burdened,
and I will give you rest.
Matthew 11:28-30 NIV

*P*anda has had a restless night. She's jumped up in bed with me repeatedly and each time she obediently gets down when I tell her to, only to hop back up within just a few minutes. Rex got up with her to let her outside, which usually solves the problem, but not this time. It's obvious that I'm not going to get any peace, so I finally get up with her. This time when I let her out, she stands on the deck woofing deep, even, single barks, at what, I don't know. It's not her typical fit of excitement announcing a visit from a neighborly raccoon, nor her high-pitched defense warning system when an unknown human is nearby. No, this is definitely different. Due to the blanket of snow and half moon, I can easily see far down the cliff into the woods, but I see only snow and barren trees. Whatever has Panda riled remains a mystery to me, and maybe even to her.

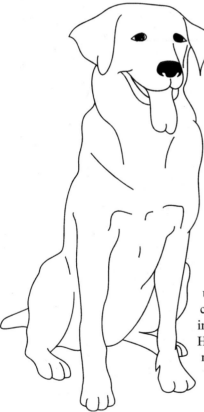

I let her back in, a blast of frigid winter air rushing in with her. We've had a cold streak plunging the temperature to zero and below for days. Panda's dogging me now, following me closely as I turn on the coffeepot, traipse to my closet to grab my terry cloth robe and slippers, and I know this means no going back to my warm bed and cuddling up with Rex. So I situate myself in my favorite living room chair, rest my achy back against a heating pad, and cover up with my mom's soft, pink throw to sip my coffee and write.

It's not long before Panda-Dear is peering up at me, patiently waiting for an invitation to take over my lap. We play our little game in which I coax and she pretends indifference, until she says, "Well, if you insist!" (No, of course, she doesn't really say this – it's printed in the little comic strip bubble above her head.) Having saved face by making me beg, she is now curled up safely in my lap drifting back to never-never land. I, on the other hand, am AWAKE! My legs are beginning to ache from her weight, but I know from experience, that in just a few minutes, she'll abandon my lap, stretch elegantly and luxuriously like a dancer warming up before a performance, and settle peacefully onto the carpet a few feet from my chair.

My mind alert for a spiritual application, I smile as I picture God curled up in a Lazyboy chair, dressed in rumpled, flannel PJs and robe, hair all matted from sleep, sipping a latte (heaven's kitchen is a wee bit more gourmet than mine). I've awakened Grace and she graciously invites me to join her, yawning deeply and rubbing her eyes as I climb gratefully into her generous lap. I realize that it is Mama-God who rises with me in the early, sleepless hours before dawn and sits with me, a comforting presence when I'm ruffled and restless. I just need to sit in her lap for a bit, just long enough to synchronize my breathing to hers, like I used to do as a little girl curled up contentedly on the sofa next to my daddy.

Just a few minutes in the lap of Grace is all I need. Quality time, PRN.

> Snuggle in God's arms. When you are hurting,
> when you feel lonely, left out, let Him cradle you,
> comfort you, reassure you of His all-sufficient power and love.
> ~ *Kay Arthur*[54]

---

54 Kay Arthur is the cofounder of Precept Ministries International, author of "Precept upon Precept" inductive Bible studies, and host of her own daily and weekly television shows. Her radio broadcasts, "Precepts for Life," can be heard at http://www.oneplace.com/ministries/precept/.

Doggone Grace

*Do not conform any longer to the pattern of this world,
but be transformed by the renewing of your mind.*
Romans 12:2 NIV

*T*he Nature of Grace would not be complete without at least one essay devoted to Grace. "Hold the phone!" you say, "This *entire* book is about grace!" Correct. But *this* essay is about *Grace*—Grace Marie, that is. A dog. A very special dog.

Always on the alert for opportunities to increase my lap time with the canine community, I found myself drawn to a "Leader Dogs for the Blind" booth at the Lion's Club Home Show (an annual event in Anderson). Year after year, I would stop at this booth to admire the Labrador Retrievers, German Shepherds, and Golden Retrievers sporting blue bandannas and blankets declaring, "Future Leader Dog." Once my nest was empty, I found myself entertaining the notion of raising one of these gorgeous, gregarious creatures.

By the grace of God, I convinced my husband to join me in this venture, and in June 2003, Grace Marie—the most adorable yellow lab on the face of this planet—came to live with us. "How on *earth* are you ever going to give Grace up?" everybody wanted to know. Good question! To make a long story short, I fell instantly and hopelessly in love with Grace—and she with me—and then in June 2004, we returned Gracie to "Leader Dogs for the Blind" in Rochester, Michigan. Following extensive training, she graduated with her blind partner in February 2005 and now lives in Costa Rica, Central America.

While Gracie was a most lovable and loving puppy, she was—well, how should I put this—a true puppy, teeny, leaky bladder, sharp puppy teeth, and all. It had been *years* since we'd housebroken a puppy. We'd forgotten what it's like to be rudely awakened in the middle of the night to the pathetic, heart-rending, irritatingly, high-pitched howls of a baby. Totally erased from our minds were the chilly treks outside to feign excitement over a few dribbles and plops, only to return to the house to clean up puddles and piles of "oops—didn't-make-it-to-the-door-in-time!" messes, as an energized whirlwind of fur whipped around us, nipping at our cold, bare feet.

Don't even get me started on the mischievous nature of puppies and their proclivities toward destruction! Gracie loved pushing our buttons and hearing us shriek, "No! I mean, 'Leave it!' (proper Leader Dog vernacular) Grace, *I said, 'Leave it!'* Good puppy! Good leave it!" When not curled up in one's lap asleep, Grace was most endearing in her "undearingness." It was hard not to laugh at her when she stole socks and "unmentionables" from the bedroom and then, with a twinkle in her eye, enjoyed to the hilt a lively game of keep-away. Panda waxed parental on these occasions by tackling Grace so we could retrieve the illicit item in question.

Gracie's most memorable heist occurred one morning when I was hurriedly preparing food and gathering up things I needed for what was to be a very busy day. As usual, I was running a tad late (okay, a *lot* late!) and for some reason, the van alarm kept going off. I made numerous trips out to the garage to stop the alarm and to load items into the van, only to discover that the van doors kept locking. I was growing increasingly more frustrated by the minute—until I happened upon Grace in the dining room, contentedly munching on Rex's remote van key. My frustration immediately evaporated and I chuckled out a less-than-convincing, "Leave it!"

I also got a big kick out of Grace eating ten of the twenty-four cupcakes I left setting on the counter to cool—they were, after all, her birthday cupcakes which were meant to be shared with her little friends at church the next morning. I fully expected a puppy tummy ache to ensue, but she tolerated the sugar orgy extremely well.

As a first-timer Leader Dog puppy-raiser, I was overly-anxious about being a good foster parent. Unlike *all* the other Leader Dog puppies that I heard fellow puppy-raisers proudly bragging about, Grace was not content to lay quietly at my feet, walk obediently by my side, or keep her trap shut in church. *"What am I doing wrong!"* I pondered anxiously, on numerous occasions. "If I were a *good* mother, my baby would be better behaved," I told myself. In time, I learned to accept Grace for who she is (active, verbal, stubborn, creative, sneaky…) and not worry about ironing out all her personality rough edges. And just between you and me, the uptight, inhibited part of me takes devious delight in Grace's antics, wishing I, too, could occasionally let myself "bark" during the sermon, chew holes in someone's favorite new sweater, or pig out on the dessert designated for company.

While I wanted Grace to become a model Leader Dog, I secretly hoped that her trainers would not be able to extinguish all of the quirks that make Grace so exasperating and yet so entertaining. In truth, I also wanted her blind partner to realize just what we went through to raise this dog for him! ("Grace can be so ornery sometimes—her puppy raisers must have been absolute *saints!*")

God seems to have a special place in his incredibly patient, forgiving heart for the quirkiest of his creation, relishing the challenge of turning tongue-tied Moses, unfaithful David, headstrong Peter, and "holier-than-thou" Paul into amazingly capable—albeit flawed—leaders. And Gracie and I are also rock-solid proof that God is still up to the task of transforming each and every one of us into one-of-a-kind gifts of Grace.

Hope

"...whither thou goest, I will go."
Ruth 1:16 KJV[55]

*H*aving successfully raised and launched Grace on her Leader Dog career, we are now busy with our second puppy, Hope, an adorable golden retriever. Her middle name is Aurelia, which is Latin for "golden." Hope is the complete opposite of Grace. In fact, I've never seen such a laid back puppy—ever! She cried for five minutes the first night when we put her to bed, but by the second night, nary a whimper. Hope is content to be in her crate. She entertains herself with her toys and her tail. She sits and contemplates. Oh, she'll rough house with Panda—and our grand-puppy, Molly—but she settles down easily and has napping down to an exquisitely fine art. She's great around kids, letting them lug her around and, basically, love her to death. Hope is almost too good to be true!

Rex and I have noticed a striking similarity between our Leader Dog puppies and our children when they were young. Matt, the inquisitive, strong-willed, active one is like Grace. Beth, our sweet little angel of a child, is like Hope. Matt loved to be held and rocked by the hour. Grace was a lap potato. Beth didn't want to horse around being rocked—she'd practically leap out of our arms into her crib at bed time. Hope can rarely settle down for a lap-nap, preferring to cloister snuggly under the love seat. Matt and Grace were mischievous and precocious. Beth was an "easy" baby, and so is Hope.

Both of our children grew up to be amazing adults (please forgive my motherly pride) and I have no doubt Hope will join Grace in growing up to be an outstanding Leader Dog. It is truly amazing how two children from the same set of parents can be so different. It's like God takes the two sets of genes, shakes them up together, and tosses them out like a pair of dice—only there are infinite possibilities, rather than a mere thirty-six. Each time he tosses those same sets of genes, he creates an entirely different human being. Rex and I birthed a redhead, a towhead, and a honey-blondhead. Each child had a different color of eyes and complexion. And their temperaments, talents, interests, philosophies, and goals are uniquely theirs. How utterly amazing!

---

55 From the cover of the Leader Dogs for the Blind Puppy Raiser Manual, excerpted from the Book of Ruth: "And Ruth said, entreat me not to leave thee, or to return from following after thee: for whither thou goest, I will go; and where thou lodgest, I will lodge: thy people shall be my people, and thy God my God." Ruth 1:16 KJV

What's even more amazing is that each and every one of us is created in the very image of God.[56] And we each have hope and a purpose for which we were created.[57]

While not created in God's image, Hope does have a definite purpose—and she will bring hope to a very special person in need. To help prepare her for her purpose is part of my own purpose in life. Together, we are the hands and feet (and paws) of Christ, helping to carry out Christ's mission as well.[58]

What is your unique purpose in carrying out Christ's mission?

56 "So God created man in his own image, in the image of God he created him; male and female he created them." Genesis 1:27 NIV

57 "'For I know the plans I have for you,' declares the Lord, 'plans to prosper you and not to harm you, plans to give you hope and a future.'" Jeremiah 29:11 NIV; "For we are God's workmanship, created in Christ Jesus to do good works, which God prepared in advance for us to do." Ephesians 2:10 NIV

58 "The Spirit of the Lord is on me, because he has anointed me to preach good news to the poor. He has sent me to proclaim freedom for the prisoners and recovery of sight for the blind, to release the oppressed, to proclaim the year of the Lord's favor." Luke 4:18 NIV

Chapter X

The Road Less Traveled

God of our life, there are days
when the burdens we carry chafe
our shoulders and weigh us down;
when the road seems dreary and endless,
the skies grey and threatening;
when our lives have no music in them,
and our hearts are lonely,
and our souls have lost their courage.
Flood the path with light,
run our eyes to where
the skies are full of promise;
tune our hearts to brave music;
give us the sense of comradeship
with heroes and saints of every age;
and so quicken our spirits
that we may be able to encourage
the souls of all who journey
with us on the road of life,
to Your honour and glory.

~ St. Augustine, 354-430 AD

There Is No Road to Grace's House

*T*homas Merton, Trappist Monk, poet, and contemplative writer, wrote a poem entitled, "There Is No Road to Grace's House." The inspiration for his poem was a picture of a house sent to him by a young child, Grace Sisson. Grace's picture was typical of many pictures created by little girls: house positioned on a hill, smoke rising from the chimney, windows with curtains, knotted trees with animals peeking out of the holes… Of course, there was a huge, brilliant sun and a sprinkle of clouds in the sky and, oh yes, a friendly, smiling dog.

My first-best-friend, Mary, and I spent hours together coloring such pictures, one after another. We were like the artists who paint for the starving artist art sales—painting essentially the same picture over and over again, with minor variations. We wouldn't stop until all the scrap paper my mom provided was converted into works of art.

> "Wouldn't it be nice if finding the road to Grace's house were as simple as doing a Mapquest search?"

What caught my attention in Merton's poem is that he mentions four times that Grace has not included a road. No driveway; no brick path winding from the picket fence gate to the inviting front door; no way at all to get to Grace's beautiful house. Merton's repetition of this seeming oversight offers implications for our spiritual walk.

Sometimes there are days (or weeks or months) when, try as I might, I feel like I can't find the road to Grace's (God's) House. There's got to be one! The Bible talks about the "straight and narrow" road to the Kingdom of Heaven: "Small is the gate and narrow the road that leads to life, and only a few find it" (Matthew 7:14 NIV). It sounds like I'm definitely not alone in my struggle!

Wouldn't it be nice if finding the road to Grace's house were as simple as doing a Mapquest search? With map and step-by-step directions, I could navigate myself right up to the heavenly mansion—with nary a wrong turn—and approach the throne of God with my complaints, questions, and numerous requests.

But could it be that there *really* is no road?

Perhaps no road is necessary because Grace knows exactly where I am and comes to me, before I even send out a distress signal. Scott Peck states, "We do not come to grace, grace comes to us. Try as we might to obtain grace, it may yet elude us. We may seek it not, yet it will find us."[59] What wonderful news for those of us who are directionally challenged!

In the parable of the lost sheep, Jesus posed this question: "Suppose one of you has a hundred sheep and loses one of them. Does he not leave the ninety-nine in the open country and go after the lost sheep until he finds it?" (Luke 15:3-7 NIV) And then—get this—the shepherd rejoices and throws a party! Isaiah, the Old Testament prophet, says, "We *all*, like sheep, have gone astray, each of us has turned to his own way..." (Isaiah 53:6 NIV) When we wander far afield and lose our way, what comfort it is to know that our Shepherd is seeking us.

Maybe no road is needed because Grace's path mysteriously intersects with, my own. "Stand at the crossroads and look; ask for the ancient paths, ask where the good way is, and walk in it, and you will find rest for your souls." (Jeremiah 6:16 NIV) I can visualize myself standing expectantly at the crossroads, where my life intersects with Grace, my eyes straining for my first sight of her.

Grace coming to me; I like the sound of that!

And Grace will come again: Hours before he died, Jesus told his disciples, "Let not your heart be troubled; ye believe in God, believe also in Me. In My Father's house are many mansions; if it were not so, I would have told you. I go to prepare a place for you. And if I go and prepare a place for you, *I will come again* and receive you to Myself; that where I am, there ye may be also." (John 14:1-6 KJV)

When I was an adolescent, we sang this scripture in choir and the verse and tune are a promise firmly planted in my heart. The morning that my father died, sitting on the foot of his hospital bed, I picked up his Bible from the bedside table and opened it to the page he had marked. Highlighted in yellow was this very passage. I surmised that only hours before he died, he read this passage, knowing that Jesus was coming for him soon.

"So, is there a road to Grace's house?" rational, inquiring minds want to know! As I ponder this question, I'm remembering the final scene in the popular movie, "Back to the Future." "Doc" (Emmet Brown, played by the zany Christopher Lloyd) has returned from the future to get Marty (Michael J. Fox) and his girlfriend, Jennifer, because, "Something has to be done about your kids!" Marty and Jennifer trustingly climb into the De Lorean, Doc's time machine. "Hey Doc, we better back up, we don't have enough road," Marty advises. "Roads?" replies Doc, as he coolly lower his futuristic sun glasses over his eyes. "Where we're going, we don't need *roads*."

Is there a spiritual parallel here?

I'll let you chew on this awhile…

59 Peck, M. Scott, The Road Less Traveled, Simon & Schuster, 1978, p. 307.

Crosspoints

Then the Lord said to him, "This is the land I promised on oath to Abraham, Isaac and Jacob when I said, 'I will give it to your descendants.' I have let you see it with your eyes, but you will not cross over into it."
Deuteronomy 34:4 NIV

*W*hen you think of Moses, what *crosspoints* come to your mind: Baby Moses floating away from captivity into the palace of the Pharaoh? (Exodus 2:1-10) The burning bush? (Exodus 3) The crossing of the Red Sea? (Exodus 13:17-14:31) Exodus 33:12-23 tells of the time when God hid Moses in a cleft of a rock and covered him with His hand so Moses could safely see God's glory. Deuteronomy 34:1-12 takes us to the top of Mount Nebo where Moses is shown the promised land—and told that he will never enter it. Imagine being Moses: A man so close to God that they spoke "face to face;" someone saved from a life of slavery and called by a voice in a burning bush to lead the Israelites to freedom. Imagine what it would be like to dedicate your life to God's service—and then be denied the opportunity to cross over into the promised land. How would you feel? Angry? Disappointed? Puzzled? Used? Defeated? Confused? Rejected? Betrayed?

Throughout life we will all have experiences when we pour our hearts and souls into a project (a marriage, a child, a career, a mission, a dream…), feeling certain of God's presence and blessing, only to have things turn out vastly different that we expected. We may feel robbed of the opportunity to enjoy the fruits of our labors and to share in the celebration. The Bible does not tell us how Moses reacted when God told him he would not enter the promised land. This is left to the imagination. We do know, however, that Moses passed the torch on to Joshua and that he was—and still is—remembered as a faithful servant of God, in spite of his shortcomings; in spite of whatever feelings he may have had at any given *crosspoint* in his life.

How have you felt when your "promised land" has not come to pass? What encouragement can you take from Moses?

Since then, no prophet has risen in Israel like Moses, whom the Lord knew face to face, who did all those miraculous signs and wonders the Lord sent him to do in Egypt—to Pharaoh and to all his officials and to his whole land. For no one has ever shown the mighty power or performed the awesome deeds that Moses did in the sight of all Israel.
Deuteronomy 34:10-12 NIV

Treasures in Heaven

Do not store up for yourselves treasures on earth,
where moth and rust destroy and where thieves break in
and steal. But store up for yourselves
treasures in heaven...
For where your treasure is, there your heart will be also.
Matthew 6:19-21 NIV

"*I*'ve never seen a hearse towing a U-Haul trailer behind it." I got a kick out of this little quip when I read it in a book being studied in Sunday school. I've always believed the "you can't take it with you" philosophy, with one important exception: books.

The way I've got it figured, God wrote a book (or at least edited it!) and as an author, recognizes the eternal value of the written word. So, my U-Haul will be loaded to overflowing with all my favorite books. While everybody else is singing lustily (is that allowed in heaven?) and strumming harps, I'll curl up on a cloud and read, while enjoying *God*iva chocolates (also something God obviously appreciates). Sounds like heaven to me!

Silliness aside, you may not be able to take "it" (whatever your particular "it" is) with you, "but you *can* send it on ahead." If you don't believe me, reread the opening scripture and see for yourself: It rings true. It's so common sense! On a spiritual level, I buy into this completely. But on an earthly, material level, I struggle to live out what I believe.

I know that material possessions do not have eternal value, yet I'm just as consumer driven as the person standing behind me in the checkout line. In the greater scheme of things, I realize money is of little consequence, really. I see this so clearly every time my health or the health of someone I love is compromised. There is no better teacher of this truth than illness or death.

I've been to the Third World and seen poverty and contentment lying down together peacefully, like lion and lamb, in the hearts of those who love God. I've lived out of a suitcase, with only a handful of books wedged in among my bare necessities, and have known the joy of being unencumbered by possessions and a "keep up with the Jones," American lifestyle. Don't get me wrong. I love material things and I don't want to give them up. But there is no doubt that the loot of my earthly life does get in the way of the spiritual lifestyle I wish to live.

Way too often, too much of my energy is focused on trying to maintain the lifestyle to which I have become accustomed. And energy spent worrying about money is equivalent, in spiritual currency, to the moths and rust that consume and the thieves that break in and steal. When I'm worrying about the stock market, I am the moth, the rust, the thief. When I bemoan how much Uncle Sam takes out of my paycheck, I'd better be checking my closets for moths, my fenders for rust.

There are no infernal tax collectors committing highway robbery on the path to eternity. I don't have to protect my spiritual assets with a security system or invest my spiritual earnings in CDs. I don't need an entourage of accountants and financial advisers. All of my "treasures" are being stored in a heavenly treasury overseen by Grace. And what are these treasures? Little acts of random kindness, great sacrificial acts of love, and a multitude of other graceful acts that fall in between these extremes: a smile of affirmation; a word of encouragement; a cup of tea and a shoulder for a distraught friend; hating the sin but loving the sinner; forgiveness; patience; endurance; a willing servant's heart; heart-felt prayer; laying down one's life for a friend…

It's not how much we have, whether materially, intellectually, or talent-wise. It's not even how we use what we have. It is the condition of our hearts and the spirit we exude that determines whether what we have and what we do with it is of eternal value. We are all expected to "bear fruit" from the measure of grace with which we have been blessed and entrusted. Whether that be a million tax-free dollars, or a plug nickel; a voice like Sandi Patty's, or the gravelly crooning of Louis Armstrong; the intellect of Einstein or naiveté of Forest Gump; the tongue-of-fire speaking ability of the apostle Peter, or the stutter of a reluctant leader like Moses.

Bearing fruit is not an option. It is a given. And to God be the glory!

Turning Back

But our fathers refused to obey him (Moses). Instead, they rejected him and in their hearts turned back to Egypt.

Acts 7:39 NIV

*W*e're all familiar with the account of Moses leading the Israelites out of Egypt, the daily menu of manna, manna, and more manna, and of how the people worshipped the golden calf while Moses met God on the mountain to receive the Ten Commandments. We've also heard countless times about the grumbling and bad attitude of the people in response to life in the desert and a daily diet of manna, manna, and more manna. The repetitive diet alone would be enough to make me want to turn back! Food is very important to me. Forty years without pizza or chocolate? Not possible!

Who among us has not "turned back" when the road has gotten tough? In reality, there are often times when it is prudent to do so. Like a couple of Christmases ago when the car carrying my niece and her husband and baby slipped off a snowy road in Michigan as they were traveling to Grandma's house. Not one of us were critical of their decision to turn back and forego attending the annual family gathering. While disappointed that they could not join us, we were greatly relieved that they were all safe and sound.

"When is forty years in the desert courageous dedication and when is it folly?"

Likewise, there are also times when it is wise to continue on. After all, we've been taught that "when the going gets tough, the tough get going!" But how do you know when to plow ahead and when to retreat? When is forty years in the desert courageous dedication and when is it folly?

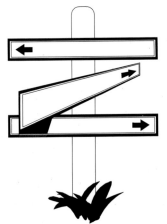

If we decide *not* to continue on, are we quitters? If we decide to go on, are we gluttons for punishment, lacking wisdom to know when to give up? Our dilemma, in the words of country singer, Kenny Rogers, is to "know when to hold 'em and know when to fold 'em." That line between wisdom and folly is *very* fuzzy. We most likely won't know whether we've made the right decision until after the fact—until after it's too late to change directions, correct the course.

I don't know about you, but I tend to expend a lot of energy second-guessing my choices. I can be encouraging a client to not be so hard on herself and then, an hour later, I'm judging myself with a torrent of harsh criticisms and negative self talk. I get impatient with God as well. Is it *really* asking too much for God to shed a little light on my dilemma and save me the agony of making the choice between enslavement to what is more comfortable or the freedom and uncertainty of reaching out into the unknown?

Even though I continually struggle to know God's will in my life, over the years I've grown to believe that God honors the sincerity and intent of my heart. Sometimes I will take the higher road and other times, when I am perhaps tired or afraid, discouraged or feeling insecure and inept, puzzled or burnt out, I will turn back, retreating from the challenges and stumbling blocks of life. That's the reality of being human. Fortunately, God does not turn back and desert me just because I'm having a bad day, shirking or shying away from responsibility, or am lost in depression, unable to recognize and utilize the gifts God has instilled in me.

So, did God turn away from the Israelites when they "turned back to Egypt in their hearts?" Would God have turned his back in disgust if they had literally turned around and beat it back to the certainty of slavery? When the pillar of cloud by day and pillar of fire by night no longer assured the weary travelers of God's presence, did God abandon them? In spite of grumblings, unfaithfulness, and blatant idolatry, God did not turn back. God will not turn back on you or me either.

Author of Our Salvation

In bringing many sons to glory, it was fitting that God,
for whom and through whom everything exists,
should make the author of their salvation perfect through suffering...

Since the children have flesh and blood,
he too shared in their humanity...

For this reason he had to be made
like his brothers in every way...

Because he himself suffered when he was tempted,
he is able to help those who are being tempted.

Hebrews 2:10-18 NIV

*D*uring Advent and the Christmas season, we are accustomed to reflecting on images of our Savior as an innocent newborn "babe, wrapped in swaddling cloths and lying in a manger." Yet this passage from Hebrews calls us to ponder how "the author of our salvation" was perfected through suffering.

"Wait a minute! Stop the tape!" we shout. "That's the video for Lent; for Good Friday! Pop in the video about the Christ Child surrounded by angels and shepherds and wise men!" We don't want to contemplate suffering right now. It's Christmas! We should be pondering happy thoughts, surrounding ourselves with "good cheer."

For many of us, though, the holidays find us in the midst of suffering. For those of us who are experiencing family conflict or separation, coping with a lengthy—or even terminal—illness, caught in the shock and grief following the death of a loved one, or perhaps dealing with depression, the image of the suffering Christ may bring more comfort than the image of the Christ Child.

In my own times of suffering, I've clung to the fact that my Savior knows first hand what it's like to suffer. It helps tremendously to know that Jesus understands my pain. So, this coming Christmas, as you set out the manger and listen to Christmas carols, take time to ponder both the Christ-child *and* our risen Savior who shares our humanity and knows our suffering. After all, the Christmas story is only the first chapter in the memoir of "The Author of Our Salvation."

Racists, Rednecks, and Bastards

This man welcomes sinners and eats with them.
Luke 15:2 NIV

*O*ne of the things I love most about Jesus is that he was a down home guy who was comfortable in the company of everyone he met: prostitutes, tax collectors, lepers, thieves, children, women, fishermen, scholars, rich men, Samaritans… As Christians, we are encouraged to strive to be Christ-like. Recently, I read about someone who emulates the Christ who "welcomes sinners and eats with them."

In the early 1960's, Will Campbell found himself in the thick of the civil rights movement in his home state of Mississippi. Due to his liberal views on integration, he was dismissed from his job at the University of Mississippi where he had served as director of religious life. Campbell became involved in leading voter registration drives and in training idealistic, young Northerners who came south to join the civil rights movement. Will Campbell befriended one young man by the name of Jonathan Daniels who stayed to help long after all the other volunteers returned to their regular lives.

Campbell found his task challenging, primarily because many "good Christians" refused to welcome people of other races into their churches and resented anyone who challenged the laws that favored white people. Campbell found his support, not among these "good Christians," but among agnostics, socialists and Northerners. On one occasion, P. D. East, an agnostic newspaper reporter who viewed Christians as the enemy, challenged Campbell to define the Christian message in ten words or less. After some thought, Campbell replied, "We're all bastards, but God loves us anyway."

Campbell's faith was put to the test when his young friend, Jonathan Daniels, was gunned down by an Alabama deputy sheriff. Daniels had just been released from jail for picketing white stores and was approaching a grocery store to use a phone when Thomas Coleman shot him in cold blood. For Campbell, this was both the darkest day of his life and "the most enlightening theological lesson" he had ever learned.

In the wake of Jonathan's death, P. D. East challenged Campbell yet again by asking him a series of questions:

"Was Jonathan a bastard?"
"Is Thomas Coleman a bastard?"

It was easy for Campbell to identify the murderer as a bastard, but he also had to admit that, theologically, his gentle friend, Jonathan, was also a bastard. Then East drove home an earthshaking lesson when he asked,

"Which of these two bastards do you think God loves the most?"

In his book, <u>Brother to a Dragonfly</u>, Campbell records, "Suddenly everything became clear. Everything. It was a revelation… I agreed that the notion that a man could go to a store where a group of unarmed human beings are drinking soda pop and eating moon pies, fire a shotgun blast at one of them, tearing his lungs and heart and bowels from his body… and that God would set him free is almost more than I could stand. But unless that is precisely the case then there is no Gospel, there is no Good News."

Following this earthquake of grace, Will Campbell became "an apostle to the rednecks." He now lives on a farm in Tennessee and spends his time among Klansmen and racial minorities, racists and white liberals. He believes that he was called to minister to the Thomas Coleman's of this world. Like Will, I pray that we each may experience an earthquake of grace that will enable us to better emulate the Christ "who welcomes sinners."[60]

"After some thought, Campbell replied, "We're all bastards, but God loves us anyway.""

60 Campbell, Will D., <u>Brother to a Dragonfly</u>, The Continuum International Publishing Group, Inc., 2000, pp. 220-224.

Walk to Emmaus

The day of Christ's resurrection:
...two of them were going to a village called Emmaus, about seven miles from Jerusalem. They were talking with each other about everything that had happened. As they talked and discussed these things with each other, Jesus himself came up and walked along with them; but they were kept from recognizing him... As they approached the village to which they were going, Jesus acted as if he were going farther. But they urged him strongly, "Stay with us, for it is nearly evening; the day is almost over." So he went in to stay with them. When he was at the table with them, he took bread, gave thanks, broke it and began to give it to them. Then their eyes were opened...
Luke 24:13-16; 28-32 NIV

I have this really great t-shirt that vividly yet simply proclaims, "GRACE HAPPENS." I love to wear it and watch peoples' reactions when they read it. I have always been intrigued with the concept of grace and for years I puzzled over the paradox of "faith without works is dead" vs. "by grace are ye saved through faith; it is a gift of God..." Ephesians 2:7-9 KJV

Not fully trusting that my actions were *not* the deciding factor in my salvation, I worked diligently at being "good" in order to avoid displeasing God and incurring his wrath and eternal damnation. As I grew in my faith, a greater part of me grew to believe that it is God's work of grace—*not* my vastly inadequate, humanly efforts—that gained me God's love and approval and assured my eternal security. But still there remained this tiny, troublesome seed of doubt that nagged in a hoarse, irritating whisper in the back of my mind: "You ain't gonna get to heaven if you ain't good!"

In May 1992, I received a megadose of grace that has pretty well hushed that joy-robbing voice. "Grace Happened" to me, in a life-changing way, when I took my Walk to Emmaus,[61] and I've been reveling in it ever since. Not that grace didn't exist before my Walk; it's just that the events of that weekend turned a flood light on grace and I saw it and experienced it in 3-D.

---

61 Information on the Walk to Emmaus can be found at www.upperroom.org/emmaus.

It never ceases to amaze me how patient and persistent God is with me. I'm a slow learner and I resist change, so my process of growth and healing often proceeds imperceptibly at the rate of evolution. Yet God does not push me or prod me or give up on me in exasperation. He meets me where I am and walks beside me at my pace. Now that's grace! And it works miracles!

"The journey we take, if it is to be authentic, cannot be a private thing between ourselves and God. ...God's grace through community involves something far greater than other people's support and perspective. The power of grace is nowhere as brilliant nor as mystical as in communities of faith. Its power includes not just love that comes from people and through people, but love that pours forth among people, as if through the very spaces between one person and the next. Just to be in such an atmosphere is to be bathed in healing power."[62]

---

62 May, Gerald G., <u>Addiction and Grace: Love and Spirituality in the Healing of Addictions,</u>
HarperCollins Publishers, 1988.

Journey Into Yes[62]

For we do not have a high priest who is unable to sympathize with
our weaknesses, but we have one who has been tempted in every
way, just as we are—yet was without sin. Let us then approach the throne of
grace with confidence, so that we may receive mercy
and find grace to help us in our time of need.
Hebrews 4:15-16 NIV

He is able to deal gently...since he himself is subject to weakness.[63]
Hebrews 5:2 NIV

*I*n May 1976, I began a long journey of saying yes to God. My husband and I had been trying unsuccessfully to have a baby. I can't describe the joy, relief and thankfulness that filled my heart when I discovered that a precious new life was nesting within me. *(Yes, Lord!)* My prayers, like Hannah's, were answered.

On January 26, 1977, Jason came crashing into our lives amid the chaos of an emergency Cesarean birth. While I lay anesthetized, doctors struggled feverishly, attempting to coax Jason to embrace life. *(Lord? What are you doing, Lord?)* That afternoon my husband's tearful report that our baby had died buried my heart in a cold chill. *(No, Lord!)*

That first year after Jason died, I felt like an emotional hurricane, with my feelings totally out of control. I don't know which was worse, my grief or my guilt. *(Why, Lord? Why?)* Even though the doctor assured me repeatedly that I did not do anything to cause my baby's death, I felt responsible. Somehow I was convinced that I had loved and wanted this baby "too much" and therefore God was teaching me a lesson: "Thou shalt have no other gods before me." *(I feel as though I deserve this, Lord!)*

When I entered the hospital once again to give birth, I was terrified. Would this child die, too, I wondered? Was I "worthy" yet of such a gift? When our second son came kicking and screaming robustly into our lives, I was elated. *(Yes, Lord! Y-E-S!)* As I sat and rocked Matthew, our gift from God, I was shocked to discover that my grief did not instantaneously disappear into thin air. *(No, Lord! I'm supposed to feel only joy now!)*

---

63 *"Journey Into Yes"* first appeared in print in the May 1994 issue of "Lutheran Women Today", a publication of Women of the Evangelical Lutheran Church in America, published by Augsburg Fortress Press.

As I parented Matt and then our daughter Beth, and as God lovingly and patiently parented me, I have come to learn a great deal about this journey of saying yes to God. It doesn't follow a smooth, direct, well-marked route. Saying yes to God in the hard times involves a process of grieving and letting go of dreams and expectations. The most difficult task for me in this journey involved letting myself feel and express my anger. Only when I was able to cry my angry tears in God's patient presence, could I move on. *(How dare you, God!)*

From a more mature vantage point on the long path to understanding, I see now that Jason's death was not a punishment from God for my lack of faith. The reality of Christ's birth, life and death began to take on new meaning for me as I experienced it for the first time as a grieving parent. *(Oh, God—the pain you endured when Jesus hung on the cross! You know my grief! Maybe…maybe I can handle this.)*

As I have healed and slowly relinquished my child, Jason, into God's arms, I have discovered a treasury of love deep within me. The fear of loving "too much" has been replaced by a willingness to risk loving freely and deeply. It is a miracle of God's love that the greatest loss of my life was transformed into a well of love from which to draw. *(Yes, Lord. I can begin to rest in you. I can see you working good from my pain. I'm beginning to see…)*

Other blessings have blossomed from this garden of grief. Having a brother in heaven made my children curious about the eternal, leading to many priceless discussions about God. The fact that I have questioned God helps me be more comfortable with my childrens' spiritual doubts and struggles. Having experienced a rocky place in the road, I trust that God will walk with my children when their paths are difficult, too. As a therapist, my own experience with grief and loss helps me be sensitive to my clients' pain.

Knowing that I could survive my own "hurricane" helps me believe that others can, too. But probably the most significant blessing has been my growing relationship with my Shepherd, who "is able to deal gently" with me, having also been "subject to weakness." My Shepherd knows and shares my pain and leads me victoriously—tentative though I may be at times—into saying yes, even in the midst of life's hurts. *(Yes, Lord. Yes!)*

Epilogue

I've come to the riverbank on this tantalizingly warm, spring-like day to write my conclusion to this collection of my Ponderings. Just last weekend, however, our neighborhood bustled with activity as residents raked, mulched, blew, and burned the most recent onslaught of fallen leaves. The dry, brown leaves crunch beneath my feet while green, leafy ground cover rises above the season's mulch, gently stirring in the breeze, pretending with me that wildflowers are, at this very moment, poking their way to the surface. Rex even spotted one wildflower still flaunting the last of its tired, purple petals. Panda bravely ventures into the frigid river for a few laps of her favorite sparkling beverage (no bottled, mountain spring water necessary for her!). She is wearing her bright orange "Don't-shoot-me—I'm-not-a-deer!" hunting season jacket—alas, a vivid reality check on my reverie.

On the bright side, this amazing Indian Summer day is a precious gift of time to make peace with the changes on the wind. We all have "changes on the wind" in our personal lives, do we not? Perched on the banks of the river of life, time flows by quietly, like the slow-moving White River here at my feet—or splashes vigorously over rocks and detours around fallen trees in the shallows that lie ahead— unconcerned as to whether we find ourselves "up a creek without a paddle."

This swan song of fall ushers in a time to snuggle up within ourselves to reflect on our relationship with God. Barren branches and the scarcity of foliage make it possible to observe sights that are hidden from our eyes in milder times. And a walk in paw-printed, newly-fallen snow always confirms that, amid the botanical barrenness, zoo-logically, life abounds. What might God want to reveal to you in the wintry, barren times of your life?

Under the decaying leaves—indeed, within this very decay—new life takes root. Just wait… You'll see!